ELIZABETH I

Elizabeth I

A GREAT LIFE IN BRIEF

BY
Donald Barr Chidsey

WILDSIDE PRESS

© Donald Barr Chidsey, 1955

TO

AUNTIE ADA

ELIZABETH I

I

THERE will always be books about this woman. Age could and did wither her (though even this process for a time seemed to fail), but custom will never be given a chance to stale her infinite variety. An analogy with Cleopatra, then, is not exact. Each was a woman who shamelessly used her womanliness not in order to gain something outside of her heritage, but rather to hold her own against fearful odds. But Cleopatra did it by *giving*, and lost, whereas Elizabeth, who *withheld*, won. There is a recent moving picture, marvelously tinted, in which Henry Tudor's younger daughter is shown questioning a schoolmaster about that same Egyptian queen. It could have happened. Elizabeth was precocious, a bluestocking. We know that she read and translated Caesar's *Gaul*, and it is possible that she read about the later campaigns. But she could not have read the play paraphrased above, for it was not written until after she died. The same can be said of most of Shakespeare's tragedies.

With the things thought of as most emphatically Elizabethan, whether in the annals of adventure at sea or those of literature, Elizabeth had little to do. When she died, Bacon was forty-two, that learned bricklayer Ben Jonson had thirty years of work ahead of him, while Middleton, Webster, Francis Beaumont, Rowley, Ford, Fletcher, were in their teens. It is true that she loved public spectacles, music, entertainments; but though it is almost certain that she saw at least some of the imperishable Elizabethan stage masterpieces, it is almost equally certain that she didn't recognize them as such, much less pay for them. A pile of poetry was written to her, some of it good, but there is no reason to believe that she actually inspired any of this. If Elizabeth hadn't been there, the poetry would have been written anyway, just as if Columbus had not discovered America somebody else would have. Elizabeth herself wrote a certain amount of verse, as did everybody in those days. It wasn't very good verse. She had many talents, but this was not one of them. She was much too practical a person to be a poet.

Nor was she farsighted, a visionary. She never dreamed of the Americas, the Indies. She starved the men on her fleets, throwing them out of work the instant a crisis was past in order to save the price of revictualing. If her admirals were great, it was rather in spite of than because of Elizabeth, who refused them gunpowder to practice with. True, she sometimes invested in short-term plunder-seeking ventures at sea, but this was no more than a rich woman's guardianship of her own money—risky perhaps, but as little risky as the weight of her royal position and an unconscionable time a-haggling could make it. If the business had its ups and downs, so did every other, for those were rocky times. The Queen, for instance, must have been furious when from his second voyage, in which she had sunk £1,000, Frobisher brought back a shipload of rock that, when tested, proved to be not gold but iron pyrites. On the other hand, Frank Drake was gone for three whole years, during which time he might have been dead as far as England knew; and when he returned, his ship was so laden with loot that Elizabeth got 4,700 per cent on her investment. There had never been such a voyage before and never was to be again. Drake was "the master thief of the unknown world." There were men who shook their heads, clucked their tongues. Not Elizabeth. While the Spanish Ambassador clamored for Drake's head, she went down to Deptford, boarded Drake's vessel, and knighted him. A pirate? Nonsense! Who ever heard of a man with a million pounds being a pirate?

She was stingy, she wasn't greedy. She would take anything that was handed to her and sometimes things that were not, and she'd cling to them; but she was no imperialist. She never went outside her own household, which happened to be England, in search of that which did not belong to her. She beat no drum for faraway conquests. She had all she could do at home.

She was fond of river travel—in part, no doubt, because of the opportunities it offered for display: the Thames was much the most popular avenue in London then, and the only one wide enough and straight enough to permit being seen at a distance—but it is likely that the vessel at Deptford was the only seagoing craft she ever set foot on. The first years of her life were spent in only a few places, of necessity. Once she had ascended to the throne, however, at the age of twenty-five, she displayed a restlessness that drove the courtiers half mad, darting from Whitehall to Hampton Court, from Windsor to Nonesuch to Oatlands to Greenwich, besides certain farther-out palaces. Every summer she spent "on progress"—traipsing around the countryside, permitting herself and her household, a matter of about fifteen hundred persons, to be entertained by this baron or that earl, who often went into bankruptcy as a result. Much of this, no doubt, was her passionate desire to appear before her people as often as possible, though some might be set down to an inherent nervousness and, as such, studied for significance. The point is, she never went far in any direction. Her passion for progresses, like her foreign policy, was a bewildering maze of stopping and starting, turning, twisting, retracing of steps, to start all over again. Almost alone among the English monarchs since the Conquest she had not crossed the Channel, nor did she ever express any wish to do so. She never glimpsed Ireland, Scotland, Wales. For all her bustle, she was never more than a hundred and fifty miles from the place where she was born.

That was Greenwich, in a room called the Chamber of the Virgins, the day Sunday, September 7, 1533, and why wasn't she a boy? Her father had wanted a boy; surely her mother, "Nan Bullen," had; and so had all of England, whipped up as the people were and worried about the succession. The courtiers were dashed, the King in a rage. Thus at her very entrance into this world Elizabeth did something unexpected—and infuriating. She had no business being a female.

The King had two children at this time, the somewhat shadowy Duke of Cambridge and a daughter by his divorced wife, Catharine of Aragon; but both were bastards, the first naturally, Mary by act of Parliament. The Duke was not to be considered as an heir, for he was only half noble and had never even *been* legitimate: Henry VIII was a precisionist in these matters. Yet ruling was a man's job. Only once in England's history had a woman, Mathilda, ruled; and this experiment had not proved a success.

The Boleyn, then, knew what was expected of her; but she failed to perform; and as months and years

Elizabeth I

crawled by, with no change in her figure, she began to lose friends. Though she had eleven fingers (the extra one, a freak, was on her left hand), still she could not hold the King. Henry soon was carrying on elsewhere, and he told her in words what everybody else was telling her with looks—if she didn't produce she was doomed.

At long last, losing patience—Elizabeth was two years and eight months old when this happened—they uncovered three lovers for Ann, one of them her brother; and all were convicted, as she was. The Archbishop of Canterbury, Cranmer, thereupon decreed that the marriage of Henry and Ann was "absolutely and entirely null, invalid, void, without force, consequence, moment, or effect at law," and Parliament declared the Lady Elizabeth—as she was thereafter called, being no longer a princess—"preclosed, excluded, and barred to the claim" (to the throne).

This being settled, there were bloody doings in the Tower yard, and the next day Henry married yet again.

Elizabeth too was a bastard now. In the eyes of all good Catholics, of course, she always had been.

It is a curious fact that, though as Queen she might well have done so, she never did arrange the repeal of the statute quoted above (28 Henry VIII). She may have reasoned that it was best to leave well enough alone. Like her father, whom she adored, she was a legalist; but there are limits even to this. For forty-five years, scepter in one hand, account book in the other, she ruled a realm that had emphatically and in the clearest conceivable language forbidden her to do so.

She never mentioned her mother.

II

JANE SEYMOUR actually did give birth to a male child, and there was great rejoicing, after which Jane died. Now it might be supposed that the malodorous old monarch, having his heir at last, would devote himself to matters of state; but he seems by this time to have formed the habit of marriage. Soon there was another wife, a German. Henry didn't like her and she did not like him. The rift was duly made legal; and then he married Katherine Howard. Like Ann, this fifth spouse was guilty, the court said, of adultery, which in the case of a queen was more than a mortal sin; it was, *per se*, treason. So they had her head off.

Then came Katherine Parr, who survived him.

Parr was herself by no means a newcomer to the married state. She'd had two husbands before Henry; and at the time he spoke—the royal request being in the nature of a demand—she had been thinking about Thomas Seymour, uncle of the little Prince of Wales. The interposition of Henry's last days only put off this plan, and she took Seymour as her fourth husband scarcely a month after Henry's death.

Katherine Parr was the only one of her stepmothers who showed the slightest interest in Elizabeth. When she and Seymour moved to Chelsea, they invited the girl to come and live with them. Her half-sister, Mary, urged her to refuse, in order to show disapproval of the indecently hasty marriage; but Mary always had been a prude. Elizabeth, lonely, accepted.

Though mankind's abhorrence may shift in emphasis from one to another as age succeeds age, most of the truly horrendous crimes—murder, cannibalism, incest—are easy to define. It has never been so with treason. So much, here, hangs on personalities, individual moral codes, precedent, the letter of the law, the law's spirit too, and of course and always the manner in which the ship of state happens to be sailing at the time.

They thought a great deal about treason in Tudor England—as well they might, their own heads being forfeit. The throne was not firm, and any change was likely to be a violent one, what was laudable in one reign conceivably being treacherous in the next. The feudal system had broken down; the idea of a constitutional monarchy had not yet been formed; and the nation was in a seemingly perpetual state of emergency. In the circumstances treason was the greatest sin, invariably punished by death. Nor was it necessary that it be proved. Accusation was enough. Trials in those days were not calculated to decide the guilt or innocence of the defendant, but only to proclaim his guilt, which was taken for granted.

Thomas Seymour almost certainly committed treason, as his brother Edward saw it. They were *arrivistes*, these Seymours, glowered at by the old-line aristocrats, and they'd scored their most palpable hit when they got their sister Jane married to Henry VIII, so that now the Seymour brothers were uncles to the King, Edward VI (the prince of Mark Twain's *The Prince and the Pauper*). They were quick to take advantage of this, especially Edward, the older, who was Duke of Somerset. Henry, wishing to rule the roost even after he was dead, had left an uncommonly complicated will. The Tudors always considered the crown of England a piece of personal property to be handed here and there as they pleased; and Henry left his kingship to his son. If Edward, then ten, should die without issue, it was to go to Henry's daughter Mary, and after her, with the same proviso, to his younger daughter, Elizabeth. Nothing was said about these last two being technically illegitimate. Henry left elaborate plans for a council of regency to rule during Edward's minority, but they were topheavy and all but unworkable. In a short time, as though by general consent, a Lord Protector was appointed—Ned Seymour, Thomas's brother. They never had liked each other, these two, and they were sometimes called, only half playfully, Cain and Abel. Now Ned *was* England; and he had some odd ideas about how the booty ought to be divided, ideas his brother did not approve.

Tom too had a title: he was the Lord Admiral. There is nothing to indicate that he did much sailing, but he had a working arrangement with some pirates who did not share Brother Edward's notions about the division of plunder. This was considered bad taste, by some even a bit criminal. Tom Seymour was thirty-eight when at last he married Kate Parr, but he did not settle down. His was a restless nature. Though his wife was rich, he sought more money, and one of the ways he tried to get this was by manufacturing it, another practice frowned upon by the government.

However, the important charge against Tom Seymour, the fatal one, was that he planned to seize the throne. It looked that way. All his actions pointed to a *coup d'état.*

We are told that he was a handsome man, and surely he had a way with him: he could count many followers, *was* counting them too. His only surviving portrait shows a somewhat stodgy personage with thin, very long, crepelike whiskers better suited to a philosopher than to a roister-doister admiral-pirate-counterfeiter.

No doubt Tom Seymour had his commendable points, but two of his faults stand out: he talked too much, and he couldn't keep his hands off Elizabeth.

Rumor said that he had proposed to her even before he proposed to Katherine Parr, immediately after the death of the King. It's certain that Seymour delighted in her presence at Chelsea. They were free and easy in those days with their physical expressions of fondness—slapping, hugging, pinching, especially kissing. All the same, this admiral who was nearing forty seems to have gone mighty far with this girl of fourteen. He used to come into her bedroom every morning in his dressing-robe, and we have it on the word of her nurse, Kate Ashley, that if Elizabeth were not in bed, "he would bid her good morrow and ask how she did, and strike her upon the back or on the buttocks familiarly, and so go forth through his lodgings, and sometimes go through to the maidens and play with them, and so forth." If she were in bed, "he would put open the curtains and bid her good morrow, and make as though he would come at her; and she would go further in the bed so that he could not come at her." When Kate Ashley remonstrated with Sir Thomas, he showed astonishment, cried "God's precious soul!" and promised he'd take his wife with him after this, which he did do. A woman of the world, the Dowager Queen thought it amusing and even helped to tickle and thwack Elizabeth. Theirs was a frolicsome family. They capered too in the garden, and it is on record that once Kate Parr held the laughing, struggling Princess while Seymour slashed her dress in "an hundred places."

Word of these Gomorrhean goings-on reached the outside world, and the mutterers who encircled Seymour closed in a little.

Katherine Parr became pregnant. This is by tradition a period of great susceptibility for a man, and Thomas Seymour seems to have been a susceptible person in the first place. It is Ashley's testimony that the Dowager one morning found him and Elizabeth in each other's arms. As they must often have been there, it can only be surmised that something about this particular position, and the circumstances, caused Katherine to esteem it beyond playfulness. The loyal Ashley herself always contended that there had been nothing "wrong." Anyway, Elizabeth quit Chelsea and took up residence at Cheshunt, a less frisky household.

The mutterers edged in.

Katherine Parr had her baby, and it died, and so did she. Tom Seymour—this time there can be no question of it—immediately proposed to Elizabeth. The circle closed. Tom was sent to the Tower.

They watched Elizabeth carefully when she got the news of the decapitation, but nobody saw her blink back a tear. Here was not a time for hysterics. On a high place, she walked a narrow way, with the lightnings playing about her feet. One misstep and she was lost.

They sent a man to examine her, Sir Robert Tyrwhitt, who learned nothing. There was no browbeating. She was near the throne, and they treated her with respect; but they were persistent.

Elizabeth went back to Hatfield, well away from the

court. She was being very maidenly indeed, living a life of determined reticence, even dressing in a nunlike manner. Yet when she learned that it was whispered everywhere that she was bearing Thomas Seymour's child, she waxed aggressive. She wrote a letter.

This woman is one of the earlier refutations of the notion that character can be told from handwriting. All her life she was erratic and unpredictable, veering this way and that, tacking, filling, but she wrote a firm, deliberate, decisive hand that was also very beautiful. She had a great deal of time to herself at Hatfield, both before and after the riotous Chelsea interlude, and she spent it in study, needlework, translations, and the writing of letters. Each letter she wrote is pictorially a work of art and fit to be framed.

Each letter is not fit to be read, however. Her speech was, or seemed to be, direct and straightforward. Her epistolary style, even making allowance for conventions of the period, is unbelievably stilted. It almost seems as if she were *trying* to be vague. She had a lot of literary learning but no literary style.

The letter written from Hatfield to the Lord Protector, the man who had signed his own brother's death warrant, is an exception. Not only is it a work of art: its meaning, amazingly, is clear.

"My Lord, these are shameful slanders," a girl just turned fifteen wrote. If anybody thinks she is with child, why isn't she called to court, where they can all stare at her day after day? She is ready. Why isn't she called?

She was not called, and she did not have a baby. One crisis was passed. There were to be many others.

III

NOBODY knew when, if ever, she was sincere. Nobody knows today. Supreme among deceivers, she deceived even herself, thus raising again the question whether a lie remains a lie after the liar has come to believe it.

Her policy now was to sit tight, to see, hear, and speak no evil. She made strides in her Latin, Greek, Italian, French. She sewed. She read. She practiced on the virginals. There were not many visitors at Hatfield. Parenthetically, she was given Hatfield outright when she was seventeen. This was her first household, and she ran it well.

Soon Somerset followed his brother to the block, to be succeeded as Lord Protector by the Duke of Northumberland, while England became more Protestant than ever and at the same time (though there is not necessarily any connection) less sure of itself. Spain, suzerain of the Low Countries, scowled from just across the Channel: Habsburgs sometimes forgave, but they never forgot, and Henry VIII in divorcing Catharine of Aragon had not only defied the Pope but insulted one of the oldest and proudest ruling houses in Europe. France, still strong at this time, before the beginning of its disastrous civil wars, scowled in much the same manner. France was four times as big as England, had four times the population, and moreover controlled the northern part of this by no means tight little island—Scotland, the "postern gate."

When Edward VI, always sickly, at last died, July 6,

1533, at the age of sixteen, there is reason to believe that Elizabeth wept. She'd not had much of a family life. Mary, seventeen years older, was a remote, glum, moody, touchy female. But Elizabeth had been close to Edward, when permitted. Once she had embroidered him a shirt. For a while they had studied together, the boy being, like Elizabeth, scholastically a prodigy. And now he was gone.

It was generally assumed that with Edward's death Northumberland would tumble, for he was a hateful man with scarcely a friend in the kingdom. But he had been given time to prepare. He may not have had England behind him, but he did have France. He had looked over two grand-nieces of the late Henry VIII, Margaret Clifford and Jane Grey (he seems not even to have considered Mary Queen of Scots, another grand-niece, who had a better claim than either of these), and selected the latter after he had managed to get her married into his own family. He succeeded in talking a dying Edward into denying the throne to either Mary or Elizabeth, something Edward had no right to do (Parliament had authorized Henry VIII to specify the succession; it had not so authorized Edward, who was a minor and incapable of making a will). Thus Northumberland was ready.

He had misread Mary. Thirty-seven, she was a small, thin woman with a deep masculine voice, a short nose, square chin, hostile brown eyes. She was given to hysterics, but she was no coward! Though Jane Grey had been proclaimed, and actually was queen for a few days, Mary rode right into London. Into the lion's mouth? It could have been.

When the dust had settled, Mary, still panting, gave

a sharp glance at Hatfield. Elizabeth was demure, her eyes cast down, all innocence. She must have known what was up, and most monarchs would have had her head anyway, just in order to play safe.

However, "Bloody Mary," except in matters of religion, was a kind-hearted, gentle woman. She disliked Elizabeth personally, distrusted her too, and had long resented being placed on an equal footing with this daughter of a commoner. Mary despised their common father, as she adored the memory of her mother, the aristocrat, the cast-off; yet it was Henry VIII that the younger Princess, twenty now, increasingly resembled— she had his laugh, his way of lifting the chin—and in public patently emulated. Moreover, though Mary still fondly supposed that England could be led back to Rome without any distasteful fuss, whatever Protestant feeling might remain was sure to rally around Elizabeth, whether encouraged by her or not. Yet Mary let the younger lady live. At Hatfield the household breathed easily again—for a little while.

Northumberland capped a career of infamy by ceasing to pose as the Protestant champion, selling out his followers, and, in a last-minute attempt to win a reprieve, announcing that he had been a Catholic all the time. He was beheaded anyway. Only *two* others were! Nor were there any large seizures of property. All over Europe statesmen gasped at Mary's leniency. Jane Grey herself was spared.

Elizabeth wore the costume of a nun. She confessed that she wavered: she asked for priestly instruction, for guidance. There were candles on the altar of her private chapel, and incense was burned there. Yet her birth, and the fact that she was next in line by the terms of Henry's will, which remained the law of the land, meant that she was bound to be the center of all sorts of plots.

There will be a great deal about plots and plotters in this book, for it was an age that reveled in conspiracy, in whisperings in doorways, in code notes, invisible ink, oaths taken by moonlight, loyalty lists, pledges, and similar dark doings. If it sometimes seems a shade childish, it must be remembered that the kingdom could have been overthrown in an afternoon, and the ins habitually were harsh on the outs. There was no Parliamentary opposition worth mentioning. All the plots were related to the succession, and one after another they misfired. Yet it would take but a single success. . . . New plots kept coming to the surface, swelling and stretching like the bubbles of a noxious marsh, exploding with a "pop," leaving a stink that lay thick on the air.

There was the Wyatt Rebellion. Almost everything went wrong, and only Sir Thomas Wyatt himself really rose, with no more than a handful of men; yet it was a near thing for a while. Mary realized now that she had to be stern. Jane Grey's head rolled at last, that of her husband too, and of course Wyatt's, and others. Sir Thomas Wyatt was a sweet singer, a poet of note. He was also a gentleman. They had him on the rack for a long while, asking him questions, but no amount of torture could cause him to implicate Elizabeth in the plot.

She didn't know this. It must have been a terrible shock to her when she was commanded to come up to London. It filled her with black despair. Here was her lowest moment, as near as she ever got to panic.

Help was to come from a most unexpected quarter—from Spain.

IV

SHE said she could not obey the summons; she was ill. The Queen sent her own physician to Hatfield, along with an armed escort. The procession spent five days on the road, traveling only a few hours at a time. Elizabeth, her body badly swollen (dropsy?), rode on a litter. It is notable that she had the drapes removed when at last the company entered London. She always did believe in showing herself.

The people gazed upon her in silence. Her hair gleamed, yellowish red; but her face had no more color than her gown: she was dressed in white, a sign of her virginity. Two rumors ran ahead of her. One was that she had been poisoned, the other that she was pregnant.

She was not long in sight. They took her to Whitehall, a royal palace then, an "official" palace, as much as any one place the seat of administration. This was Whitehall before Inigo Jones was put to work on it, and it could scarcely have been a place of luxury. In the heart of London, it was a businesslike structure, even its grandeur being conventional, somewhat self-conscious. It was without gardens. Elaborate enough (it had been York House), still it had none of the charm of the country palaces Elizabeth particularly loved—Greenwich with its pleasant park, its forest; Oatlands, a sleepy domicile; unassuming Nonesuch—though it did have in common with these the fact that it was situated on the river, a fact that might have been ominous. Londoners loved their river in those days. It was their principal playground, a place for parades and bright display. Yet a royal person, a princess say, might well reflect that the Thames also led to the Tower of London.

At Whitehall, then, she demanded to see Mary. This was refused. Nobody paid homage to her, or even called to inquire about her health. She was a prisoner in her own rooms, and they were not very good rooms. She was awakened late one night and commanded to dress. To go where? The question was not answered. She must dress immediately, and she must come alone, without her maids. She said good-by to those maids. "Pray for me," she told them, "for I know not whether you will ever see me more."

She was told that she was to be sent to the Tower. She demanded again to see her half-sister, and again was refused. She insisted at least that she be permitted to write, and she did write Mary a long letter, passionately and perhaps even honestly protesting her innocence. The letter was not answered.

They approached the grim pile from the river, and she entered it, after a near-breakdown, after some tears of true despair—Elizabeth was never a weeping woman, except that she sometimes used to weep with rage—by the Traitors' Gate. Few who went in there ever came out alive. Elizabeth did. Yet even when she was transferred, some months later, Mary refused to see her and she was not told where she was going. Again she traveled by river. Under a tall, gentlemanly, if somewhat confused knight, and a guard of soldiers, she was for months shifted from this house to that, obscure and for the most part uncomfortable places out in the country. She was watched all the time, her servants severely limited. She was not allowed to send or receive mail.

The situation got better slowly. There was no abrupt

change. Frightened, she played her part perfectly; but that she owed her life to Philip there can be little doubt.

He was not at this time Philip II, but he was the favorite son of the Emperor Charles V, and it was understood that soon, when Charles retired, Philip would become King of Spain and overlord of the Low Countries. He had been raised with this in mind. Everything he did or said, and doubtless everything he ever thought, revolved around this fact. No man was ever more conscious of his position, his fate. No man was ever more serious about it.

Philip is miscast as our villain. There was nothing sinister about him. He was a man of little imagination, no sense of humor at all, a bookkeeper destined by birth to rule half the world. Called *El Rey Prudente*, he liked to do everything himself, down to the tiniest detail, not trusting deputies or secretaries; and he was an excruciatingly slow worker.

Central Europe was to be his brother's heritage. Western Europe and the Indies were Philip's own. He was to be lord of more land than any other man who ever lived (always excepting his own father), but there is nothing to indicate that he took any interest in the far-flung Americas, to him mere sources of money. Like Elizabeth, whom he in no other way resembled, Philip had a parochial mind. Potentially, then, Spain was the wealthiest country in the world; actually she was one of the poorest. Her armies were easily the best, crack troops maintained at great cost in other lands, and her navy the biggest. Millions were poured into Spain, but they went right through, spreading out over all Europe, where prices skyrocketed as a result. On the other hand, the Low Countries, roughly what is now Holland and Belgium, were prosperous—and his. France would gulp them in a moment if she dared, and their recovery, even if possible, would take untold treasure and men. But France would not dare move if across the Channel her traditional enemy, England, was allied to Spain.

This was Philip's problem. His father had thought it all out for him. Even his method of attack was characteristic of his family. The Habsburgs never used force when they could use matrimony instead, and they had married their way onto some of the best thrones in Europe.

So Philip let it be known that he was willing to wed Mary. He did not seek to rule England. But he did wish very much *to rule the ruler of England.*

Mary was dazzled. She thought that nothing could be finer than this match, unworthy though she was, and she would have liked to accept the offer instantly before Philip could change his mind. England was not so sure. There was no notable prejudice against Spain in England, where the thing to do was hate France; and all the responsible councilors were agreed with Mary herself that a king of some sort was necessary, a man trained to this kind of work, which a woman could hardly be expected to do alone. Nevertheless, your Englishman is by nature suspicious of strangers. To Mary's dismay, the most dependable of her councilors insisted on making terms, a treaty—a careful one, too.

That such an insignificant nation should presume to hestitate about an alliance with Spain surely must have stabbed Philip's pride; but he knew his duty, to which he was a slave, so he acceded. Catholicism was coming back to England, though not at all with the glad speed Mary had expected—the Emperor himself had peremptorily ordered Cardinal Pole, the Papal legate, to postpone his return to England, his native land, an order that astounded Mary—and the matter of the Mass, all-important a little later, was amicably arranged. But the restrictions were to be many. All sorts of conditions were laid down. Philip (whose father created him King of Naples and King of Jerusalem for the occasion, just so that nobody could say Mary was marrying beneath her station in the matter of titles) was to be proclaimed King of England, and any children he might have by Mary were to succeed to the throne, but he himself could not rule if he outlived his wife. This hurt; but Philip was patient. He was always patient. His patience is one of the great phenomena of history.

It was the Emperor again who, after talking it over with his son, solemnly interceded in behalf of Elizabeth. Spain needed this match. Elizabeth was a heretic, true, but she was intelligent and might yet be won to the True Church; and meanwhile it was advisable to keep her, if only as a sort of reserve.

To this an eager Mary agreed. Mary would have agreed to anything to get her bridegroom.

So Philip sailed. There had been processions, proclamations, parades, and many Masses, blessings, ennoblings—in short, all manner of celebration—for weeks before the stupendous event. There were almost a hundred vessels in the wedding flotilla, all of them gorgeously decorated. The great standard on the flagship itself was of crimson damask painted with the imperial arms and with golden flames, and it was thirty yards long.

V

HE landed in a downpour of rain. Even so, in black velvet and silver lace, with his curly yellow beard and his close-cropped fair hair, with the massive gold chains around his neck, and with all his gems and the Garter Mary had sent him, he must have been a bright sight. He was not so well attended as he would have liked. On one pretext or another, and sometimes without troubling to give any excuse, the English had forbidden large numbers of the Spaniards to land. This piqued Philip, who attached much importance to the size of his entourage—his tail, as the Scots used to call it. But he bore it. The men he was permitted to take ashore had been coached in the parts they were to perform. There must be no incident! This too galled Spanish pride, but it was for the glory of God, as Philip himself pointed out. *He* was all affability, though he couldn't speak a word of English, and he did not even wince when for the first time he faced his bride. Small, somewhat swart, with a dumpy figure, and speaking and laughing in a deep, disconcertingly masculine, nervous voice, she had tiny suspicion-lit brown eyes that contrasted with eyebrows so slight and light as to be almost invisible, giving her an incongruous air of astonishment. But Philip was a Habsburg, and this task too was for the glory of God. He couldn't have behaved better.

Still the English did not like him. They feared that he planned, despite the treaty, despite all his personal protestations, to draw them into a war on the Continent, which as a matter of fact is exactly what he did plan.

They resented the very presence of the Spaniards in the streets, in taverns, everywhere. There were many rufflings.

London had been scrubbed for the occasion, parts of it painted and otherwise cleaned up: all the rotting heads were taken off the pikes on London Bridge, for instance. Philip avowed that he was ravished. He certainly didn't like the weather; and he seems to have been shocked too, probably disgusted, by the English habit of promiscuous kissing; but once again he said nothing. He and his bride talked in Italian, as Mary knew no Spanish.

Philip has gone down in history, English history anyway, as a bigot; but he wasn't. It would be wrong to say of him that religion came first, politics afterward, or the other way round; for he saw politics and religion as one and the same thing, inseparable. Though he came from the country of *the* Inquisition, he had nothing to do with the Smithfield burnings and other acts of persecution that were to win his wife her sobriquet. On the contrary, he advised caution, moderation; and it was in this connection that he was so gracious to the Lady Elizabeth. Go slowly, he urged. They'll come back to the fold if you don't try to force them.

Mary was hurt (Philip could have been too, though he was less loud about it) when Parliament, otherwise tolerably obedient, refused to return any of the Church lands seized by Henry VIII, or to pass legislation that might permit the Church to try to get these back by any other means than an appeal to the consciences of individual owners—an appeal that did not prove effective. Yet more than greed prompted this refusal. The truth is that even a partial restoration would have upset the whole national economy, and, of more immediate moment, it would have cost the lay peers their predominance in the House of Lords, an important body then.

England was Catholic, officially, but it was not as it once had been; nor would it ever be again.

From the beginning, for all the treaty protections, for all his own careful hands-off policy, Philip ran the royal household. Mary, who worshipped him, turned over to him every responsibility he'd consent to accept. He was not happy: she must have known that. His heart was on the Continent. Two things above all he had sought in England, had condescended to marry Mary for—an heir to the English throne (his son Don Carlos had been specifically barred from this by the terms of the marriage contract) and an army. It was his cautious custom never to crack a smile, yet even his somber features must have relaxed for a moment when in November of the year 1554 Mary announced that she was pregnant.

This almost certainly would ruin Elizabeth's chances of getting the throne. More, a good healthy baby, of whichever sex, would remove Philip's only reason for urging toleration of the reserve heir, Elizabeth. Indeed, the erasure of the lady at Hatfield would then be more pressing than ever, for putting her a peg lower on the succession scale would stimulate the Protestants and political adventurers to even more desperate measures. Courtenay, through whose veins ran the bluest blood in England, after the Wyatt Rebellion had been kept in the Tower for only a short time and then (conceivably because he had "squealed": it is sure that he was one of the first to break down) had been shipped off to the Continent, where he was allowed to wander around a little, not much. A joining of his house, Devonshire, with that of Tudor had for years been a fond hope of the plotters. This kind of plotting, however, Philip could understand—and counteract. He found Elizabeth a husband.

There was nothing new here. Elizabeth, like any other princess, took the marriage block for granted. She was only a few months old when her father opened negotiations with Francis I for her marriage to the French King's third son, the Duke of Angoulême, also a baby. These came to nothing. Nor did the negotiations for a marriage with Lord Arran, heir of the house of Hamilton, second to the Scottish throne, when Elizabeth was nine. Philip himself at seventeen—Elizabeth was eleven then—had been mentioned as a possible bridegroom. Ivan the Terrible had proposed from afar. The King of Sweden had put forward his heir apparent, Eric. Additionally it had from time to time been suggested that Elizabeth be allied in wedlock to some member or other of the houses of d'Este, Ferrara, Saxony, Medici, Arundel, and Westmoreland.

And of course there had been the impetuous Tom Seymour.

Excepting Seymour, these suitors had been safely distant. Philip's candidate was different. Philip produced him.

Emmanuel Phillibert of Savoy was young, good-looking, head of one of the oldest ruling houses in the world. There were only two things against him: he was poor and he was a foreigner. His vast estates, a principality, had recently been seized by France, and war seemed the only way to get them back. Philip was at war with France, therefore he and the Savoyard were allies. Philip had his heir now, or thought he had, but he still sought an army. Phillibert sought the same thing.

The military reputation of the young Prince was excellent, so were his connections. All he lacked was a country. So Philip ordered the marriage.

It is a pity that we do not have details of this transaction. Elizabeth was perhaps the greatest master of the art of evasion that this world has known, and her pet particular province, where she shone the brightest, was the evasion of matrimony; so that her earlier practices in this field would make a fascinating study.

She said no. Though she protested that she was overwhelmed by the honor, her answer came down to this unroyal assertion: she wouldn't marry a man she had not met.

Philip must have been flabbergasted, but for once he acted with alacrity. He invited Savoy to London, summoning Elizabeth as well. He supposed that if these two met face to face, romance, which he had doubtless heard or read of, would do the rest.

Elizabeth said that she was ill. Peremptorily Philip bade her come. After all, he was the King. She went.

We do not know whether she and Emmanuel Phillibert ever did meet. Perhaps Phillibert was too impatient: impatience can be flattering, but here was a lady who never liked to be hurried. The Prince champed, eager to be off. All too clearly, the marriage bed to him was going to be but a springboard to the battlefield. Elizabeth had other ideas. Moreover, she was sure that she had gauged public opinion accurately: she was always sure of this, and usually right. However imperious her mien might become, she never failed to keep a wetted forefinger raised in order to learn which way the political wind was blowing. She couldn't risk a foreign marriage now.

Cornered, she came out with it. There was a scene. She was bullied, but she stood pat. She was sent back to Hatfield. When this business was over, when the Queen had borne their son, or even their daughter, if it so pleased God, *then* Philip would take care of this recalcitrant waif, this child of a strumpet.

VI

MASSES were held, and parades, and prayers were offered in honor of the child to come. Cannon were loaded, flags brought out, ambassadors were commissioned and their suites picked, official proclamations were framed. On April 3 came the announcement—*a boy!* The cannon were discharged, all over the kingdom bonfires were lighted, *Te Deums* sung, people got drunk. The ambassadors started away—but were called back. No, it wasn't a boy. Horrors, a girl then? No, not a girl, and not a monster either. In fact, no baby at all. The announcement had been premature, a misunderstanding. In another day or two. In another week or two, in a month, the nation still was waiting on tiptoe. Then folks got disgusted. The last to believe what the physicians for some time had been telling her was Mary herself. It was not until August that she admitted she was not pregnant. She never had been.

Trying to hold a man by saying that you carry his child is one of the oldest wiles known to womankind, but Mary I had no wiles. Whatever her shortcomings, she was as honest a person as ever lived. There is not the slightest doubt that her condition was hysterical. Probably she had the physical symptoms—swelling of the abdomen, stoppage of the menstrual period. She may have thought that she felt life. Though especially inconvenient in a queen, there is nothing rare about the condition, certainly nothing new. The Greeks some thousands of years ago called it pseudocyesis, the very word we use today.

Weary, Philip went away. He had lingered only out of politeness, pretending to believe in his wife's pregnancy. From Brussels he wrote putting forward reasons why he could not get back at just this time. He kept advising moderation.

It would have been well if Mary heeded this advice. She had been savage before; she seemed insane now, a woman obsessed. She was genuinely shocked at the resistance she had encountered in bringing England back to Rome. Her mind, never strong, may have become unhinged. She threw away her earlier popularity, caused in part by her personal courage as displayed in the Jane Grey and Wyatt troubles, in part by her leniency to political offenders. In a few short years she became the most hated person in England—always excepting her husband and his Spaniards, who, it may be, got out of the country barely in time. People said that the Inquisition was being transplanted to England, and they blamed Philip first, but blamed Mary too. This was unfair. The persecution of Protestants was never anywhere near so bad in England as in virtually every other European nation outside of Scandinavia. Still, it was the worst England had ever known. Nor was there anything furtive about it, or anything to indicate that its fury might abate. On the contrary, it seemed to glory in its own bestiality. The burnings were made as slow as possible—nobody was ever quietly garroted first, as was done in Spain from time to time—and they were of course public and attended with great fanfare. At first only bishops or priests were hauled to the stake, but soon there were other victims, lay victims, mere boys, women. The Church went further, and caused the bodies of past offenders to be dug up and mutilated and burned in public.

This sort of thing, far from intimidating the public, set it to muttering. The martyrs went to their fates well, appearing to be conscious of the importance of the roles they played. "Be of good comfort," the aged Latimer said to his fellow bishop, Ridley, as they were being led out to the fires, "we shall this day light such a candle, by God's grace, in England, as I trust shall never be put out." He was right. They did.

Hard times didn't help. It was not Philip's fault that crop after crop was poor and there was famine in the land, but doubtless he was blamed for that too. It was popularly reported that if he ever came back, it would be at the head of an army of Spaniards by means of which he'd overrun the country, making every Englishman a slave.

When Philip did return—with only his accustomed entourage of three hundred-odd—it was after nineteen months abroad, and even then he did not stay long. Perhaps he didn't dare to. Mary tried to hold him, but her grasp was weak, she was failing. She learned after he had gone that she was "pregnant" again, and had this officially announced; but nobody but Mary herself took it very seriously this time. It turned out to be just what everyone had assumed, another case of pseudocyesis.

Plots were exploding like firecrackers all around the throne, and the people "only waited for a drum." This was what came of entrusting the government to a woman —and to a damned foreigner. When the Throckmorton plot was exposed, Throckmorton himself actually was acquitted, and the crowd in the street cheered him. In a rage, Mary had the jurors jailed.

Catching a fever in Padua, Courtenay obligingly died, thus relieving some of the pressure on Elizabeth, whose name had been linked with his so often as to form a plot pattern.

Sir Thomas Stafford landed on the coast with a handful of harebrained followers, seized Scarborough Castle, and held it for two days. His purpose, he proclaimed, was to prevent Philip from invading England at the head of a Spanish army. Thirty-one heads fell as a result of this exploit, but Elizabeth's name, wonder of wonders, was not even mentioned.

Still, who could know what was going on in Mary's dark brain? Hatfield House was being visited by some of the leading statesmen and most astute politicians of the period, and the Queen, who had never trusted her half-sister, must have glowered. Elizabeth did what she could to keep the callers away. This was a lesson in loyalty, one she learned well. She could still lose. One misstep on the part of some well-intentioned fool might mean the block.

Mary would not see her. Mary went on signing death warrants. There were uprisings in Cambridgeshire, Kent, Essex, Sussex, Hertfordshire, Warwickshire—local affairs, easily put down, but not without significance. The Navy had deteriorated. There was no gold in the treasury. The string of forts, built at enormous cost for the protection of the coast, stood unmanned. Philip kept writing for money, and somehow, not always legally, his wife got it to him. Parliament didn't like this, and neither assuredly did the people. The muttering rose almost to a roar.

It was no time to lose Calais.

This was known as "the brightest jewel in the English crown," though it's hard to see why. The last physical reminder of the Lancastrian wars, it gave some sort of justification to the English monarch's official claim to be King of France; but it was not much of a place. Incorrigibly French, so that a large and expensive garrison was needed, it could never be supported by its hinterland. It would always be more trouble than it was worth, except sentimentally; but then the English are a sentimental people.

True, its loss was a humiliating defeat, one that greatly strengthened the hand of the French in the forthcoming peace dickerings. It made a popular hero of the strongest and most bitter enemy England had in France, the Duke of Guise. Worst of all, it might have been avoided; for the attack, though audacious, was by no means a tactical surprise, and even after it had been taken the town might have been retaken if the English had acted fast. The mess that was made of this showed the world how weak England was.

"When I die," Mary said, "they'll find 'Calais' written on my heart."

She did die soon after this, a pitiful old thing in pain, at Whitehall, November 17, 1558. The Spanish Ambassador, de Feria, didn't wait for the event. He got on his horse and started for Hatfield. He had plenty of company on the road. All kneel to the rising sun!

VII

SHE was twenty-five, a woman of medium height who looked tall by reason of the way she stood. What her figure was like it is hard to say, for the farthingale made any female look like a trussed chicken balanced on a bell; but she did have a fair complexion, a good breast, good hands, and—presence. You knew when she came into the room. She had a disconcerting habit—it often jolted ambassadors meeting her for the first time—of lifting her chin and with both hands pushing back the collars of her dress, exposing more than was considered seemly even in those days. She used to do this as though the heat oppressed her; and perhaps it did. She was a *hearty* person. Whether this was all natural or whether much of it was an attempt to imitate her father, whose popularity still was immense, it is impossible to say. At any rate, when she laughed, as she did often, she laughed all over. She seldom wept except in rage; but her voice could become a screech, and she'd waggle a bony forefinger and hurl curses like javelins. Sometimes she might hurl more, as on the day she took off a slipper and threw it at Walsingham, a man she never could abide.

She was more temperate at table. The custom of three rather than two daily meals was just coming in, and Elizabeth accepted it. Yet in that gluttonous age she was a pecker, a bird, and except on ceremonial occasions she seldom took a drink. She stayed up late, she got up early. All her life she was fond of hunting and dancing, the latter then the more violent sport. She was undoubtedly very ill when summoned to testify about the Wyatt Rebellion, but this passed. She sometimes pleaded illness when she sought to get out of an interview that might be unpleasant, but who doesn't? She had a bad attack of smallpox in the fall of 1562. This passed, leaving no notable marks. She was the despair of her physicians, who fussed around her: she hooted in derision at them. Frederick Chamberlin, in a lay-medical study of Elizabeth, insists that she suffered all her life from this ailment or that, and more than hints that the reason she never married lay in her knowledge that she had inherited syphilis. There is no proof of this.

The heritage we know she did get was not so handsome as at first glance it might appear.

Only one bishop consented to anoint her at the coronation ceremony, and he did so, he said, in the hope of averting civil war. England had a state religion, but nobody was sure what it was, and Elizabeth herself had no firm convictions. She was impatient of the whole business. No doubt the liturgy and discipline of the Roman Church were less obnoxious to her than the dourness and sourness of Calvinism. Yet the Calvinists were loyal. They might be disagreeable, they might talk through their noses, but they'd stick to her, having no place else to go. By the very nature of her position, by her birth, she almost had to be a Protestant; the Pope could be lenient, however, when he dealt with a prince, and perhaps a dispensation might yet be arranged. There is good reason to believe that Elizabeth dallied with this notion for a while.

Nobody can ever know what the proportion of Catholics and Protestants was; some Catholic claims go as high as 95 per cent, some Protestant claims as high as

80 per cent. In the west and north there were whole counties where you couldn't find a Protestant, where feudal conditions still prevailed. On the other hand, the seaports and manufacturing centers of the south and east were definitely and increasingly Protestant, London overwhelmingly so.

When Henry VIII broke with Rome, as we all know, he seized the monastery lands, and much has been made of this by the Catholics, as well as by the old-time aristocrats, who fumed to see power—for land was power then—pass into the hands of upstarts. Henry sold about two thirds of these lands, leasing the rest, and he spent the proceeds on war in France. The two protectorships under Edward VI, with their cabals and cliques, their internecine strife, had been extremely expensive. Mary, her conscience troubled about the monastery lands, gave liberally to her Church out of her own pocketbook, the family's, the royal exchequer; and she dispatched untold sums to Philip for his war on the mainland.

When Mary was near death, she sent word to her half-sister that she would do nothing to oppose her succession to the throne, only begging Elizabeth to keep the "old religion" and to settle her, Mary's, debts. Elizabeth has been adversely criticized for going back on the promise about the "old religion," if she made such a promise. A safe assumption might be that she only made soothing sounds, sounds calculated to help a broken, dying woman feel a little better. She certainly never committed herself in writing.

Elizabeth did, however, in time, settle Mary's debts. These amounted to upward of £20,000. But this tells only part of the story. Not only was the country in bad shape financially, but the money that did exist had been passed through a series of debasements, so that now nobody knew where he stood, and England's credit abroad was low.

There were three different kinds of pounds, for example, with three different values attached to them, even without making allowance for the prevalence of "clipping." By far the commonest coin was the tester, or sixpence. Some of these were made of metal containing 8, some 6, and some 4 ounces of silver to the pound avoirdupois; these were in fact equal in value, being worth about 4½ pence, as the difference in fineness was balanced by the difference in weight; they had originally been issued as shillings. But there was also a tester—and the average man couldn't distinguish it from the others—with silver of a fineness of only 3 ounces to the pound; this was worth about 2½ pence. There were laws to prevent taking advantage of these differences, but they worked about the way such laws always have worked.

All of this was offensive to the housekeeper, Elizabeth, a tidy person, who set about correcting it.

What is known as Gresham's Law—that bad money drives out good—was so named three hundred years later in honor of an Elizabethan, Sir Thomas Gresham, founder of the Royal Exchange. Until Gresham's time it had been supposed that the opposite was true—that good money drove out bad.

Let it not be forgotten that Elizabeth stood alone. She had no organized party behind her, not even a definable group. She had no near relations, brother, sister, cousin, uncle, aunt. Her subjects, who numbered about five million, just at the moment were cheering themselves hoarse; but what would they be doing tomorrow? She had no real friends. She'd never had a chance to make any.

What she did have was courage. She was to need it.

VIII

THIS was the situation: France was afraid that England and Spain would get together, England was afraid that Spain and France would get together, while Spain was afraid that France and England would get together.

Spain was the strongest, England the weakest by far. If a fight started, all three would be in it; and each strove to arrange matters so that he would be on the two-side rather than alone.

The German states, just beginning their career as a military manpower pool, were for the most part still busy snarling at one another; and except that some were on France's flank, and that two or three did now and then rent out armies, they might almost have been marooned on the frozen steppes of Russia. Much the same was true of Denmark and of Sweden.

Complicating factors were the Low Countries; Ireland, with which both Spain and the Pope were soon to flirt; and Scotland, a ramp for invasion, cheek-by-jowl with the Catholic northern counties of England where Elizabeth was not loved. By long habit Scotland was allied with France, and right now was governed by a Frenchwoman, Mary of Guise, as regent for her daughter, Mary Queen of Scots.

His father had laid two injunctions upon Philip: he should at all costs keep the English alliance, and he should stamp out heresy everywhere. How he was to do both these things at once was not clear. His Ambassador to England, de Feria, had called early to remind Elizabeth, in gravest tones, that she owed her crown to Philip.

She had answered that she didn't at all, she owed it to the English people. De Feria, outraged, wrote to his master that smooth words were never going to be enough: Philip should talk to this nation only with "sword in hand."

Philip did not agree. He hated war, an appallingly expensive business even for the heir to all the Indies. Then, too, it might take a little time to flatten those island people, and that time could conceivably be used by France to swoop upon the Low Countries.

No, not war. Philip had a better plan. In one of history's funniest letters, he wrote to de Feria that, despite Elizabeth's deplorable religious convictions, despite demands on his own time, and the expense, and also the danger that it would mean war with France, still he believed that "in the general interests of Christiandom" he should sacrifice "my private inclination in the service of our Lord, and . . . marry the Queen of England." De Feria was to inform Elizabeth of this gracious decision. Of course Elizabeth would turn Catholic and would apply to the Pope for absolution "for her past sins." And Philip must not be expected to spend much time with her, for he was a very busy man. Finally, he could not consent to a clause in the contract similar to that in his contract with Mary, providing that the Low Countries be a heritage for the oldest male issue of this proposed union. Such a clause, Philip feared, would be prejudicial to the interest of his son by his first marriage, a nasty little epileptic named Carlos.

Before he broached the subject in audience, de Feria showed this letter to some of the maids of honor, and word of it, perhaps even a copy, got to Elizabeth.

She did not say an outright no when de Feria put it to

her in formal fashion. Elizabeth seldom did say yes or no straight out, with no equivocation; her "answerless answers"—the expression is her own—already were famous. But anything less than the eager acceptance of this offer was an affront to the dignity of Spain, and de Feria's face was purple as he bowed out.

The very next day, January 15, 1559, she was crowned. It is of course a great show, and it never had a principal more keenly aware of this fact. The Mantuan envoy and certain other foreigners thought that Elizabeth lacked majesty, smiling too much of the time, waving too often; but the people loved it. They repeated many times the story that the Queen had giggled and said that the anointing oil stank.

Soon afterward Philip married a sister of the King of France—and Elizabeth was furious.

Philip himself did not get to the wedding, but delegated as his proxy that goat-bearded Quixote-turned-tough, the Duke of Alva. The bride's name, incidentally, was Elizabeth. There was a big celebration, culminating in a tourney, as part of which King Henri II tilted with Count Montgomery de Lorge, captain of the Scotch Guard. Thick-thewed, this Henri, if somewhat thin of brain. He had spent his boyhood in Spain as a hostage, and in temperament, though not in blood, he was more Spanish than French, a man of dark and violent passions. For some time he had been glowering at England. His oldest son, the Dauphin, was married to the girl-queen of the Scots, Mary, whose grandmother, Margaret Tudor, had been a sister of Henry VIII of England, a fact that gave Mary an excellent claim to the English crown. As she was already Queen of Scotland and was soon to become Queen of France, it might be supposed that Mary would not press this other title. Recently, however, her uncles, the dreaded Guises, had talked her into quartering the arms of England with her own. Elizabeth had protested promptly, and now she waited. Would the device be withdrawn? The answer came at the tournament, where the English arms were embroidered on the throne hangings, on the breasts and sleeves of the heralds, everywhere. It was nothing less than a public announcement of Mary's pretensions.

Things might have gone badly for England, then, if Henri had survived that tilt with the Count Montgomery. He didn't. The Scot aimed for the casque, something only a fool or an expert would do, and he hit. The end of his lance was snapped off. A splinter reached the King's brain. Henri died ten days later, July 10, 1559, and his death was to make a great difference in this story, specifically and immediately introducing into it two extraordinary women.

Mary has been mentioned. She was now Queen of France. A great-granddaughter of Henry VII of England, she became Queen of Scots at the age of one week when her father, James V, died in a fit of vexation after the Battle of Solway Moss. She was five when they sent her to France to cement the Scottish-French alliance by marrying Francis, the infant Dauphin. Now she was seventeen, but though the marriage had recently been consummated, she was not a mother. She was a favorite at the French court. It is customary to call queens beautiful, but this one really was.

Henri II's widow, Mary's mother-in-law, was Catherine de' Medici, daughter of a fabulous but by no means ancient Italian banking house. She had no difficulty getting herself acclaimed regent. Catherine was the complete villain, a *diavolessa*, or she-devil, who smiled and smiled. Often called Madame la Serpente, she was singularly unsnakelike in appearance. An ambassador described her as "a tall stout woman with a red face, hair that looks like a wig, pale eyes, big mouth, and a rough way of speaking, almost like a peasant woman."

There were only three parties in France in those days, and Catherine de' Medici the bland, though she steered a crooked course, kept as much as possible to the middle of the stream, staying between the ultra-Catholic Guises on one side, the Huguenots on the other. Like Elizabeth, she believed that religion should be kept in its place.

So it was that, despite the prejudices against females in high places, a Spanish woman, the Duchess of Parma, ruled the Low Countries as viceroy; a Frenchwoman, the regent Mary of Guise, ruled Scotland; an Italian woman ruled France; but the woman who ruled England remained what she had always been—English.

IX

NONE the less, it was a man's world, the English court. It numbered about fifteen hundred persons, preponderantly male. There were perhaps twenty ladies. There were not even many female servants: the scullery and the buttery, for example, were in the hands of men, and men were the cooks. The courtiers had some sort of private life. The Queen had none. Nor did she permit her maids of honor to have any; for though she treated them like naughty girls, she expected them to behave like vestal virgins, and nothing would so quickly put her into a pet as a love affair near her person. Thus when Sir Walter Raleigh got the Throgmorton girl into trouble, no amount of poetry, passionate pleading, or political pull could save them. They married; but all the same they were thrown into the Tower, there to spend six months. Thus too when it was revealed that Lady Catherine Grey, the late Jane Grey's younger sister, had made a secret marriage with Lord Hertford—which ceased to be secret when her figure gave her away—they were clapped into separate parts of the Tower. There the baby was born. And there a year or so later, love having laughed at locksmiths, or perhaps bribed them, *another* baby was born, which threw Elizabeth into a frenzy, while the world guffawed.

Much has been made of this prudish attitude on the part of one who certainly was not a prude in most respects. Possibly Elizabeth thought it her prerogative as queen; or she may indeed have esteemed herself the most beautiful woman in the world, so that an interest in any other woman after a man had once beheld Elizabeth might be construed as an insult. Shrewd in many respects, still she could absorb any amount of fulsome praise. Part of this, true, was of the period. Here was a rodomontade age. Yet Elizabeth went far beyond the conventional coyness, and she simpered at the most sticky outpourings of poetic treacle, afterward archly fishing for more. Did she really take it seriously, as she appeared to do? Or was she laughing up her sleeve all the while? We shall never know.

She *may* have been a dirty-minded maiden who hated to think of any other female having the pleasure she couldn't or wouldn't, while she wheeled tremulously around the flame of the ultimate intimacy, horrified, fascinated. At the same time, it is well to remember that Lady Catherine Grey was a near claimant to the throne, a Protestant too, while Hertford, oldest son of the late Edward Seymour, came from a family notoriously avid for power. Even supposing that these two young things were genuinely in love, their marriage, secretly performed, was an act of treason.

As to the maids of honor, they were chattels, wards of the Queen, property for which she was responsible. Each literally represented an estate, so many acres. They were to be disposed of as Elizabeth thought best. They had no right to dispose of themselves. The Queen might undo any marriage performed without permission, though in fact she seldom did this. The system was rotten? Elizabeth did not make the system, which was passed on to her intact.

The same thing applies to almost every part of the government. Prices were rising all through this period, as gold and silver flooded in from Philip's fabulous lands to the west. Everything cost more. Salaries of court functionaries, however, stayed the same: there simply was not enough cash to raise them in proportion as the expenses of the posts were raised. The inevitable result was a system of winked-at bribes, regularized if unauthorized fees. Elizabeth made no effort to reform this, for she was not a crusader; but neither did she make it worse. Her court was corrupt, yes, but it was not gangrenous. Indeed, as courts went, it was comparatively clean.

Immediately around the monarch there were fifty gentlemen pensioners who constituted a sort of guard of honor. On ceremonial occasions they must wear, at their own expense, full suits of armor, and then each carried—or, more often, caused a servant to carry for him—a gilded battle-ax. Their principal duty was standing around. Thus they assembled at nine every morning in the presence chamber to greet the Queen when she appeared and accompany her to chapel and back, and they repeated this performance each evening. When she rode, they alone were supposed to help her on and off her horse. They were, in fact, a sort of exclusive club, not easy to get into.

The actual working guard numbered about four hundred, half of them paid, the other eager youngsters who served without pay in order to be near the center of things. They wore uniforms. They carried halberds. Their captain did not need to do much with them, for they were well organized and more or less ran themselves, but his was a position of great glitter, though of almost no political importance. In consequence the captain of the guard was likely to be one of the more decorative knights—Dudley, Hatton, Raleigh, Blount.

Since Elizabeth had to feed this whole organization,

even when she was on progress—for they all went along with her then, pitching tents with identifying banners in the countryside around small places where there weren't enough inns, so that they suggested a medieval fair—the kitchen staff must have been enormous. Cecil, who noted down everything, listed one of Elizabeth's meals, just one, presumably typical (but it must be remembered that a dozen or more maids of honor would finish this off after Elizabeth had picked her dishes in private, and then *their* maids would be fed): six kinds of domestic poultry, eight varieties of wild fowl, seven kinds of meat, custards, tarts, wardens, etc., four gallons of beer, three pints of wine. Cecil computed the cost at £6. 10s.—say $600 today.

There were some 275 horses in the royal stables, and about a hundred men took care of them. Once Elizabeth tried to cut this down a bit, but she failed: the steeds really were needed. Possibly seventy-five men had charge of the hunting and hawking equipment. The Queen was fond of both these sports, but she would in any case have had to maintain such facilities if only for the entertainment of ambassadors. The gardening staff of twenty-odd seems absurdly small today, in proportion. They did not go in much for gardening then. There was a medical staff of thirteen, for though the Queen might scoff at physicians, not everybody in court felt the same way.

Her father and grandfather had maintained fools or jesters, and her successors, the Stuarts, were to revive this custom, if somewhat self-consciously. Elizabeth would have none of such nonsense. There was always God's plenty of laughter in her court. She could see no reason to pay for it.

The master of revels, a personage, might have as many as a couple of hundred men working for him at one time. His workshops turned out a continuous series of triumphal arches, painted drops, plaster statues, masks, costumes, floats. This was not a theatrical group. It put on set pieces, spectacles, not spoken drama. Elizabeth never had her own company of players, as did Leicester, Southampton, the Lord Chamberlain, King James, and others.

Finally, she always had within call musicians to the number of those found in a modern symphony orchestra. There was some kind of music going on somewhere all the time in every palace Elizabeth occupied. If they didn't play, or if in playing they lagged, she'd scream at them. Their numbers varied, and most were foreigners, chiefly Italians. At a given time there might be five or six sackbut-players, two or three players of the virginals (an instrument at which Elizabeth herself was an adept), a couple of recorder-players, a bagpiper, some flutists, trumpeters, drummers, an organist, several harpists (even these were men!), some lute-players, some rebecs, many singers.

For all this, she got a lot of work done. This was because she had a good council. Above all, she had Cecil.

There was no cabinet, in the modern sense. The privy council was an approximation, but the differences are important. There were cliques, cabals, but not a stable, classifiable group. Not until more than a hundred years later did parties with names, with avowed purposes and accepted leaders, coalesce. Members of the privy council were appointed directly by the Queen, and were of course removable by her. Their votes, *as* votes, did not count. Often Elizabeth, when she did not wish to say yes or no, would plead in public that she must be guided by what her council said; then, after a swift fierce aside, making clear which decision she wished, she would dump the problem into their laps. Not always did they oblige. They had integrity. They played politics, necessarily, and on the whole they were in accord with the Queen's wishes; yet they were not men of straw. From time to time Elizabeth would curse them, though not so vehemently as she cursed Parliament and the Convocation. She never attended their meetings.

The council was always in being. It had the power to call before it anybody it wished. It was responsible, as a body, to nobody but the Queen. Its debates usually were secret, and they were informal. Almost every privy councilor who was not a peer—about half were not— was a member of the House of Commons, not because of his councilorship but by regular election. Hence they had much to say in Parliament, though they could not be haled before the Commons *as* councilors and made to answer questions as cabinet members are today.

The most outstanding difference between the privy council and a cabinet lay in the fact that no councilor was assigned to a specific task. Some—the Lord Chancellor, the Lord Privy Seal—were members by reason of these positions, but the positions gave them no rank or relative place inside the council itself. There was no minister of this, secretary of that.

The body, born in Norman times, by now had lost much of its judicial authority, though it still sat in the Star Chamber. Likewise, though the Lord Treasurer was a member, the council as such no longer had much to do with finances. Its functions were advisory and administrative. Its duties were many, its responsibility great. Because of her fondness for hunting and hawking, for dancing, music, cards, late hours, Queen Elizabeth impressed visitors and newly arrived ambassadors as a frivolous woman, and the wonder was expressed in many a letter home that England survived at all under the rule of anybody so slipshod. This was unjust. She worked hard. She might be laughing, mouth open, head tilted high, but she was taking everything in. And she knew how to delegate authority—something Cousin Philip never learned. The council could carry on foreign correspondence; it could receive and dismiss ambassadors, even declare war; but it knew that the Queen was near at hand, her head cocked, her eyes open.

There was never a limit to the size of the council. Under a weak monarch it might be strong, under a strong monarch weak. As from time to time it grew in size, there would come into being an inner core of knowing ones with whom alone the prince communicated: this was in very truth the privy council. Then it would be cut again. In the reign of Edward VI the privy council was too large to be efficient, and much too noisy. Under Mary it got even larger, swelling from nearly forty to nearly fifty. Elizabeth trimmed this to manageable proportions, not by any abrupt measure, not drastically, but quietly. Perhaps for the first time in English history, under her the council contained no churchmen. She didn't care for these. "My bishops are a pack of knaves," she used to say. During most of her reign the council appears to have numbered about eighteen to twenty members. Perhaps eight or ten of these attended the average meeting. There being no constitution, no quorum ever was called for. There might be as few as four or five present.

Easily the best of Elizabeth's privy councilors, who

had been one of the first and was to stay almost to the end, who if there had been a prime minister would have been that prime minister, was a man in appearance the least "Elizabethan" of the lot. William Cecil was short, thick, pale-eyed, close-mouthed, furtive. He suffered from gout. He was interested in genealogy, gardens, and staying alive. As he saw it, there were two sides to every question, often more. This does not mean that he was indecisive! But he was careful. He left as little as possible to chance. Pondering each problem separately, he would column the pros on one side, the corresponding cons on the other, after which he would study them. Like as not he would turn this table in with his own recommendation. Once his mind was made up, he could be stubborn. Politically he was flexible until such time as the vote was taken: he was accommodating, but consistent, persistent as well. When he needed to, he could be slippery as any eel. He had served as personal secretary to each of the two Edwardian protectors, but as each was decapitated, this sly man somehow managed to save himself. He must have been mighty uncomfortable for a while when Mary got the throne, but he retired to his estates and quietly turned Catholic—and was spared. This has been held against him, but nobody thought anything of it at the time. Many a higher-placed person did the same —the Lady Elizabeth, for example. "May the earth open and swallow me alive if I be not a true Roman Catholic," she had cried once; and the earth hadn't.

Cecil was not greatly rewarded. Nobody grew very rich under Elizabeth. A favored few were permitted and even encouraged to make a splash, but she kept them in control. Robert Dudley, Earl of Leicester, the most pampered, died owing his sovereign a considerable sum.

She undoubtedly had loved him as much as ever she could love any man; nevertheless she got her money back: she kept selling his estates until she did.

A dumpy, lumpy figure, no ruffler, no mustache-twirler, Cecil moved about with solemn face in that glittering company. He must have been laughed at, but he was feared by more than a few and respected by all. He got things done.

Once in 1566, when she had a Parliamentary joint committee before her, trying (unsuccessfully) to get them to quash a bill, she scolded them *en masse* at first, then some of the more conspicuous ones individually, mincing no words. To Dudley: "You, my lord, you! If all the world forsook me, I thought that you would be true!"

"Madam, I am ready to die at your feet!"

"What good would that do?"

Elizabeth was right. She was surrounded by men who were willing to die for her. William Cecil was different. Cecil would live for her.

Posterity has formed differing opinions of Cecil. There are those who esteem him a diabolical influence, the power behind the throne. To others he was an old fuddyduddy.

The latter version, surely the further from the truth, might have been launched by William Shakespeare. Cecil died in 1598, and at about that time his instructions to his younger son, the carefully trained hunchback who was to become the first Secretary of State, were published. These instructions contain much good, sound advice, but undeniably they have a certain fussbudget air. A snigger rose from the sophisticated when first they saw the light of print. Did the Bard take advantage of that? It seems likely. *Hamlet* was first produced in 1601. Polonius is a sinister rather than a silly figure in the early versions of the story. Shakespeare may have known a clown who could get a great deal out of just such a part, and may have pitched it accordingly. Whatever the facts, it is certain that the popular imagination, directly then, somewhat less directly since, has seized upon William Cecil as the original of Polonius, a meddlesome old fool who deserved to be stabbed behind the arras. This is misleading. Cecil was a bore surely, but he was a man to watch.

X

ELIZABETH's grandfather and her father had fretted about Scotland, trying to conciliate that cantankerous country; and this made it a family obligation. As far back as anybody could remember, certainly as far back as the Conquest, it had been obvious that England and Scotland, needing each other, should be combined for administrative purposes. The question was how to go about it. The Plantagenets had tried answering this in a characteristic way—with armies. But if Scotland was not hard to take, it was hard to hold. Again and again the hordes from the south overran the lowlands—they never tackled the highlands—only to find that they could not keep what they'd captured. In the late thirteenth century Edward I tried another method when he offered his oldest son, Edward of Carnarvon, to the girl-queen of Scotland. But she died before arrangements could be made, and King Edward with a sigh turned to arms again and spent the last twenty-odd years of his life surging across Scotland, backing away, surging across it again.

Henry VII, the first Tudor monarch, also tried matrimony; but, a skinflint, he haggled so hard that the dowry was whittled down to a sum scarcely more than an insult—and Henry didn't even pay all of that! As a result, Elizabeth's Aunt Margaret had had a hard time of it in Scotland, being almost constantly engaged in efforts to raise money, and at last she went to England to live with her brother, Henry VIII, who didn't like her. It was Aunt Margaret who had given the Stuarts their claim to the English throne. Her son, James V, married a French girl, the beautiful Mary of Lorraine, and their daughter, Mary, now Queen of France as well as Queen of Scots, was in addition calling herself Queen of England. The situation became even further complicated when the boy-king of France died, leaving Mary a widow at seventeen and a dowager queen. She then not unnaturally decided that she had better go back to the land of her birth. Yes, to the English it was clear that something should be done about Scotland.

Bribery suggested itself, for it was a practice not considered shameful then, and the Scots, being poor, were peculiarly susceptible; and though expensive, it was less expensive than war. But bribery of the Scots was a Danaidean task. Elizabeth never could be sure that she was bribing the right parties: it sometimes happened that by the time the money got there, another combination of nobles was in power. In such a case, not only was the original gold not returned, but a second set of hands was extended, the palms up. Even a spendthrift might have found this disconcerting. It drove Elizabeth wild. Moreover, no matter how high she went, France, so much richer, could go higher. To break that old alliance with France, to drive the French out, was Elizabeth's primary problem. She couldn't risk war. Whatever she did, she would have to do in an underhand way.

Matrimony? It was a possibility that was of course considered, and the man most often mentioned was the Earl of Arran, heir of the house of Hamilton. If Elizabeth could be wedded to him, their child would have an excellent chance of uniting the thrones, and immediately the Queen's prestige in Scotland would be greatly enhanced, for there were many Protestant nobles there who favored such a match, Arran being a rabid Calvinist. Well, Elizabeth said, she'd look at him.

Arran was in France then. Catherine de' Medici, through her son Charles IX, immediately ordered that he be arrested, alive or dead. This Scot could knock the props out from under Mary's throne before Mary could get to Scotland, and Madame la Serpente was eager to get her daughter-in-law out of the country.

Cecil's agents, however, smuggled Arran into Switzerland and later into London in disguise while Elizabeth blandly assured Catherine that she knew nothing whatever about it. Even after she had met Arran at Cecil's house and talked with him for several hours, Elizabeth swore to the French Ambassador that she hadn't heard of his rumored presence in England.

One look was enough. Doubtless the bleak austerities of his theology also repelled her. Anyway, she wouldn't have him. We know little about the personal appearance of Arran except that he was short, swart, beetle-browed, truculent of mien; but his intellectual shortcomings were notorious. At this time he was considered no more than, say, "eccentric." In a few more years he was to be declared unquestionably and legally lunatic.

Elizabeth didn't tell *him* that she was turning him down. She put him off with half-promises, gave him a bag of money, and sent him, still in disguise, to his native land, where from the family castle at Dumbarton he was to direct the Protestant anti-French movement.

The French were bottled up in Leith, a small force but a good one, incomparably better soldiers than those who besieged them, and better led. It was known that reinforcements had been sent, but these were scattered by a storm.

Then Elizabeth did a thing that was to set a pattern for her. She sent a fleet to blockade Leith, instructing the Admiral, young Sir William Wynter, that he was to stop the arrival of French reinforcements in any way he saw fit. She added bluntly that she would not stand back of him. In other words, if he got into a fight and was captured, he would be hanged as a pirate, and his Queen wouldn't lift a finger to save him. Wynter went anyway, and he did a brilliant job.

Elizabeth fooled nobody then, nor did she when at last she was obliged to send soldiers to the siege. She explained these "volunteers" in various ways. First she denied all knowledge of them; then she intimated that they had slipped across the border without her consent; finally she insisted that the anti-French Scots weren't in rebellion at all but were simply trying to protect themselves against an invasion not of the French but of the followers of the house of Guise, and that she, Elizabeth, was trying to help them. The essential truth of this third assertion gives the reason why Philip did not interfere. If the French were not ousted from Scotland, they might, under so spirited a queen as young Mary, move down upon and take England. Philip couldn't risk that.

This was the first appearance of these "volunteers," who were to become familiar on the mainland.

The regent, Mary of Lorraine, died. The French capitulated at last, with all honors, and sailed away, never to return. There was no war—at any rate, no openly acknowledged war. Just at this time the Huguenots were pushing forward in French public life, and the house of Guise, the *politiques* too, couldn't venture a war. This was not a stroke of luck for Elizabeth. She had been secretly encouraging the Huguenots for some time, sending them money, all the while protesting publicly that she had never done anything of the kind.

Cecil was sent to Scotland, where he negotiated a diplomatic triumph. The Treaty of Edinburgh won virtually everything the English had fought for, even though they hadn't fought much, and it satisfied the insurgent Scots, whether properly rebels or no. The only party not pleased was France, which, teetering on the verge of civil war, was in no position to give voice to its resentment.

The Treaty of Edinburgh stipulated that Mary Queen of Scots, just then in Paris getting ready to return to the land of her birth, should disclaim her rights to the throne of England during the lifetime of Elizabeth. This clause was to cause more trouble than all the rest of them put together. It was to cost many a life.

Mary temporized, not refusing outright, but not signing either. She applied to her "dear sister" Elizabeth for a passport to go through England on her way back to Scotland. There is little doubt that she did this only in part through curiosity—to see what Elizabeth looked like—and chiefly because she could imagine the figure she'd cut on progress through England, and particularly in the northern counties, the Catholic counties. Elizabeth wrote back to say that the passport would be forthcoming as soon as the Treaty of Edinburgh was signed. You didn't talk to Mary Stuart like that. She took a ship for Scotland.

Meanwhile Elizabeth had changed her mind and dispatched a letter saying that Mary could pass through England, after all. But the Queen of Scots had already gone when that letter arrived—gone to her fate.

XI

THE UNANIMITY with which it was assumed that no woman could reign alone in England is amazing. The entire kingdom, Catholic and Protestant alike, took it for granted that Elizabeth would get married. Individuals and then a committee from Parliament approached her on this subject. At first she said (or seemed to say) that she meant to be wed, and then she seemed to say (or said) that she didn't. What she really had in mind we shall never know.

Even if she put it off for a few months, couldn't she, the Parliamentarians wailed, name her successor? Only one life—the life of a superlatively lovely woman, but still, one woman, one life—stood between them and civil war. They kept pointing this out.

"Do you think I could love my winding-sheet?" she cried.

She had seen, in those years at Hatfield, how courtiers turn toward the rising sun. She needed every bit of power she could get to run this country properly. A designated successor, even if unwillingly, would divide it.

Yet the promise of a marriage, the negotiations—these were titillating and at the same time could be useful. She was the best catch in Europe, and she knew it. There was no time when she was not toying with the possibility of some husband. She was a monumental flirt.

Eric of Sweden tried again, and again was rejected.

Two sons of the Emperor Ferdinand, younger sons, archdukes, were proposed at the same time and without mention of preference. "Which one am I supposed to marry?" asked Elizabeth with a roguish smile. Politically she could not have done better, as she realized. The house of Habsburg was the traditional ally of England, yet its current representative in Spain, Philip, fresh from his unfortunate affair with Bloody Mary, was unacceptable. She had offended Philip's pride when she turned him down. A union with the eastern Habsburgs might heal that wound. It would straddle France; it would keep Spain, and hence the Low Countries, quiet; and it would infuriate Mary of Scotland. There were other advantages. For years she was being pressed to wed one of the archdukes, either one. She demurred, but kept coming back to the subject. She never did say no, and she never said yes either.

Ferdinand was a bigot, also something of a milksop. Charles was more moderate in his religious views. It was not likely that Charles could be won over to Protestantism, not right away anyway, but he would not be offensive to the English public. Such a match could be counted on to keep the Catholics in check.

Elizabeth asked questions. What was Archduke Charles like, then? Well, he was an amiable, agreeable lad, undoubtedly healthy, not bad-looking at all. It was true that he had an excessively large head and (a grave fault, with fashions what they were) was bow-legged; still he was a fine figure of a man. Elizabeth would have to see him, she said. She did not trust portraits or word-of-mouth descriptions. Let him come to England.

Now, archdukes are not to be summoned like servants. The Emperor did not trust Elizabeth. How could he be sure that Charles, if permitted to go, would not be rejected? It would make fools of his whole family.

The Emperor was as eager as the friends of Elizabeth to make the match. Like his nephew, Philip, he was under orders from the now-dead Charles V, to keep the English alliance at all costs. Nor was he horrified by the tales told of Elizabeth, who could be mighty careless about certain matters, nor about her Protestantism: the Habsburgs in Vienna were being almost indecently lenient just at this time. All the same, the Emperor said that the Archduke couldn't go.

Into this discussion Catherine de' Medici now thrust herself. What about her oldest son, Charles IX, for Elizabeth?

Catherine clearly sought to embarrass the archducal negotiations and at the same time make it difficult for Elizabeth to deal so openly with the Huguenots. Another thing that she might get out of this proposal was the breaking up of a match in the making between Mary Queen of Scots, her daughter-in-law, whom she hated and feared, and Don Carlos, son and heir to Philip of Spain. *That* marriage was one Catherine did not feel she could permit. Parenthetically, Elizabeth herself was going after Don Carlos with every trick she knew, hinting to de Feria's successor, the wily and always entertaining Bishop de Quadra, that she might like to hear a suggestion from that quarter. De Quadra pointed out that as she had already refused Philip, it was taken for granted that she was not interested in Philip's son. Well, she replied with a sigh, perhaps she had been thinking over that refusal. Her cousin of Spain had been precipitant about finding another bride after she, Elizabeth, had shaken her queenly head. He might have waited a little. . . . She could have gone on with that sort of thing for years, as de Quadra knew. Don Carlos was never offered to her. She wanted him, clearly, to keep Mary from getting him, not for the lad himself, a singularly obnoxious person.

Elizabeth pretended that she did not take Catherine's offer seriously, but Catherine persisted. Wasn't he somewhat young? asked one Queen. He was growing, the other retorted. Charles IX was a boy with a morbid imagination and poor health. He had nightmares, even in broad daylight. He wrote poetry. Now fourteen, he was about half Elizabeth's age—and not much more than half her height.

At least one person, De Foix, the French Ambassador in London, was taking these proceedings very seriously indeed. Elizabeth's shilly-shallying—he was new on this job and had not got used to Elizabeth—set him atwitch. Why, he cried, she had already taken eighty days to make up her mind whether to marry Charles IX, whereas the whole world had been made in only six. Elizabeth replied that the world had been made by a greater artist than herself. She had always been irresolute, a weathervane, she confessed. It was her greatest fault.

All this, and more of a similar sort, was not made any the easier by the fact that the lady was in love.

XII

WHAT she could see in Robert Dudley nobody has ever been able to make out. They were the same age, having been born on the same day—even, they would sometimes gigglingly confide, at the same hour. They had been childhood friends; more, they had occupied adjoining cells in the Tower at the time of the Wyatt uprising. Finally, though perhaps it should be first, Dudley was handsome. He cut a flashy figure. Sussex, who despised him, called him "that gypsy." Portraits do not show him swarthy: perhaps the reference is to his fondness for trinkets and bright ribbons. He was an incorrigible show-off and spent money in the grand manner—as well he might, considering the way Elizabeth heaped him with monopolies and other special privileges.

All through the land the parvenus preened themselves. Johnny-come-latelies strutted in palace corridors. Fortunes were being founded while the ancient feudalism crumbled into dust. It was a time of change in almost everything—art, fashions, poetry, the drama, swordsmanship, eating habits, architecture, methods of warfare, geography, religion. The whole world, but especially the microcosm that was Elizabeth's England, was convulsed by a revolution, and it was no more than natural and even proper that "new men" should come to the top.

Elizabeth herself approved, though she kept them well in hand. She was chary of giving titles, honors. When in '72 she had Norfolk's head off, that was the end of the last duke in the land, and she created no other. Of course there were no princes; and Lady Catherine Grey, withering in the Tower, her husband taken away from her, was called Lady Catherine, never princess. Elizabeth, though so brilliantly served, raised few to the peerage. She did not create many knights; and when later, after certain battles, a few politically ambitious youngsters like Essex used their right as commanders in the field to bestow the accolade upon dozens, even scores of their own personal followers, the Queen bitterly rebuked them. The sneaping blast of her sarcasm was such that many a man truly was afraid to vaunt his brand-new "sir" when he came to court, counting it rather a demerit than an honor. As for the title *baronet*, this did not exist in Elizabeth's time: it was invented by her successor, James I.

Even among the "new men" Dudley was disliked. He had toadies but few friends. He headed no party, represented no principle. Ambassadors fawned upon him, and his household was the largest in the land after that of the Queen; yet all this was not because of any outstanding service or special abilities, but only because Elizabeth smiled his way. In the religious differences that reft the land he took no stand; and it could be that this attitude alone won him favor with the Queen, who hated religious extremism.

Nor should the taint of treason, provided it showed as a single spot, ruin any escutcheon then. Most of the very best families had lost a member at some time on the scaffold on Tower Hill; not to have a convicted traitor among your ancestors was almost like not having a Crusader. The Dudleys, however, despite their recent emergence, seemed fairly to make a tradition of treason. "Dear Robin's" father *and* grandfather, not to mention sundry uncles and cousins, had died on the block. It was not a background likely to recommend itself to any queen. But Elizabeth forgave all.

Although Dudley had ridden near her in the coronation procession, another was favored as suitor in the earliest days of the reign. This was Sir William Pickering, who had come back from the Continent at the news of Bloody Mary's death. Pickering was thirty-six, handsome, well set up, a great hand with the ladies. He gave himself airs, dining alone, virtually boasting that he'd soon be king. The sporting men agreed. There were bets on record of as high as four to one that Pickering would get the throne. He never did. Somehow he faded away. Maybe he had overdone his act. Maybe it was just at this time that Elizabeth was smitten by the Dudley charms. Whatever the reason, Dudley was soon in the ascendant—and he stayed there.

It was generally believed all over Europe that they slept together. Elizabeth herself was in part to blame for the slander, for she flirted outrageously in public with Dudley, had him in her private chambers at all sorts of odd hours, and in general behaved like a woman who didn't care for her reputation. Again and again it was reported that they were married. Various great houses were named as the scene, various bishops as the agent. Today we are convinced that there was no marriage *or* affair. In 1562 when she was seriously ill with smallpox and sincerely of the belief that she was about to die, Elizabeth begged the assembled councilors to create Dudley a peer, make him protector of the realm, and grant him £20,000 a year. She swore at that time that there had been nothing improper between them.

She recovered from the smallpox and never mentioned the protectorate or the proposed pension again; but she did not recover so readily from her infatuation with "the gypsy." It almost drove her ministers mad. They never knew what to expect.

One day a relative of Dudley sought an interview with the Spanish Ambassador, de Quadra, and circuitously suggested that if Philip could persuade the Pope to bless the arrangement and to regularize everything, Dudley and the Queen might get married and bring England back into the Roman Catholic fold. This was an oblique way to put forward a proposition that could be called world-shaking; but Elizabeth usually moved obliquely.

Bishop de Quadra, cautious, said he'd have to have the proposition straight from Dudley. Soon he was so receiving it. Dudley indeed made more than one such visit. He who a little later was to head the puritan faction at court now protested fervently and repeatedly that, provided his and Elizabeth's terms were met, she and he alike would do anything Spain and Rome asked. Even allowing for the *esprit d'escalier* that lights all of de Quadra's letters, the ring of truth is here. *Elizabeth never spoke up, to be certain.* It never got that far.

This same de Quadra found himself in another position of embarrassment at about this time. It happened afloat. Many of the royal palaces, many other large houses too, were on Thames. Persons of the court spent much of their time getting into or out of boats, a semi-aquatic life, virtually Venetian. Elizabeth loved it—not because there was salt water in her veins, as certain fatuous fools have suggested, but because it was the best way to show herself to the crowd. Often she received petitions or heard informal pleas while embarking or disembarking. It was at a landing-place that young Walter Raleigh, according to a tale that's probably not true, cast his cloak upon the mire before her. Those who were invited to go aboard her own barge on a watery occasion were honored. She used these invitations, as she used everything, for political purposes. De Quadra then, Spain being in favor at the moment, was aboard the royal craft. What's more, he shared the poop with Elizabeth and her master of horse. Elizabeth was in high good humor, as she always was when in the eye of the populace, for she saved her sulks for smaller places. She and Dudley joshed one another like playful children, squeaking with laughter, while the Ambassador-Bishop pretended to pay no attention and in truth understood little of what they said. De Quadra, however, came to attention when Dudley put forth the suggestion that as he was right there, and *they* were there too, why didn't he marry them on the spot? Elizabeth, all giggles, protested that perhaps de Quadra did not know enough English. "I let them trifle in this way for a time," and then he read them a little lecture; or, at any rate, so he reported to Philip II. It is certain that he performed no marriage ceremony—certain too that even he, who knew her so well, was not sure what Elizabeth might do about Dudley. She had confessed to de Quadra, on another intimate occasion, that she had her private thoughts about the man, adding darkly that she was "no angel."

An unimaginative soldier, a weak and erratic statesman, hopeless as a businessman, Lord Robert Dudley nevertheless could be useful. Such was the glitter of his official and unofficial positions alike that it was necessary to take him seriously; yet the Queen could always deny anything, asserting that Robin had been acting on his own. Never before, however, had she been so extraordinarily secretive. Even Cecil didn't know the details, didn't know anything for sure, and was frantically trying to find out.

The reason nothing came of it, the reason the marriage could no longer be considered, was that a woman was found dead at the foot of a steep stair in a house otherwise unoccupied; and nobody ever was to know whether she fell or was pushed.

All this while, it must be understood, Robert Dudley had a wife. The marriage to Amy Robsart years before, when they were both in their teens, had not turned out well. Amy stayed in the country, chiefly at Cumnor Place in Berkshire, never going to court. She wasn't often even mentioned; and when she was, as the Elizabeth-Dudley flirtation maelstromed, it was darkly predicted that she wouldn't live much longer, she'd be poisoned. This talk in itself was not important. Folks were always referring mysteriously to poison in those days. It was the Italian influence, the Renaissance, the late Borgias. Poison, in truth, was not often resorted to in England, the English being too straightforward and direct for that sort of thing.

In this case the poison stories have an exceptional interest just because they were so rife immediately before the day when poor Lady Dudley was found with her neck broken at the foot of that staircase. The Queen herself was reported to have said something to the effect that Amy Robsart, who hadn't been well, would die soon.

It was a queer case. We don't know whether the lady was poisoned and *then* pitched downstairs, as many preferred to believe, or whether her death was due to that broken neck. There was an inquest, but it was pretty thoroughly hushed up, thanks to Dudley's influence. Nobody had witnessed the crime, if there was a crime, all the servants having been sent to a local fair for the day —by Lady Dudley's own order, they testified—but nobody even hinted that Dudley himself might have been there at the time. His behavior after getting the news was a bit odd, and he didn't go to the inquest, but that may have been only nerves.

There was a third possibility, in addition to the fall and the push hypotheses: she might have jumped. It was she who had sent the servants away. She had been ill for some time, and she was lonely out there, forbidden the court, and unhappy.

Whatever the truth, it was clear to Elizabeth that now she couldn't marry dear Robin. The world preferred to believe the worst, and it would be years before she and Robin could live this down. They didn't drift apart. But it was a long time before the Queen thought seriously again of marrying the favorite, and by then she'd passed the crisis: she had recovered her senses.

It is perhaps not too much to suggest that that poor woman with the broken neck at the bottom of the stairs, regardless of how she got there, had saved England from another bloody revolution.

XIII

THE IRELAND of Tudor times has been likened to a bankrupt estate that owner after owner tosses to his heir, pleased at least that *he* has put off for a bit the inevitable day of reckoning. It was a heartbreak house, the graveyard of military as of political reputations. Elizabeth's policy in Ireland was stupid, cruel, expensive, confusing, indeed anarchic, and almost incredibly shortsighted. It was a policy or lack of policy which she had inherited, and which she made no move to change.

There were flare-ups with the emergence of superior Irish figures, a Fitzmaurice, a Shane O'Neil; and there were noisy and messy affairs to obtrude upon the attention, such as the massacre at Smerwick; but for the most part during Elizabeth's reign Ireland, if not quiet—it was never that—was manageable. Only toward the end, when Spain and the Vatican began to interfere, did the situation become, from Elizabeth's point of view, serious.

The truth is that Elizabeth never paid much attention to Ireland.

Scotland was different. It was nearer; it was stronger; it was having its own Reformation, a violent one. Though no Frenchman remained, it had a tradition of friendship with France which might readily be renewed. Also, it had a queen.

The subject of Mary Queen of Scots is to be approached with caution. No other heroine in history posthumously called forth so many champions. Mary Stuart was a great woman. What *kind* of great woman she was, whether she had too large a heart or none at all, will always be argued. Certainly the Mary who ruled Scotland from August 1561 to June 1567 was by no means the wan, exquisite prisoner of later years, a martyr. Mary in her early twenties was lively, lovely, brilliant, strong, a prodigious horsewoman. She was not formal in her manner: she didn't care for ceremony. She appeared to be simple, direct, though in fact she was preternaturally cunning and could strike like lightning. Her energy was tremendous, her scruples hard to find. After all, she'd spent her life in the last Valois court, an institution that shone and stank "like a rotten mackerel by moonlight," the court of which Brantôme, the *Fair and Gallant Ladies* man, was the Suetonius, the Petronius. She may have been maligned; possibly she was not wicked, only careless. In any event, she was no pushed-around puppet but a wide-awake woman who played the game as she found it—and played it extremely well.

It was an extraordinary predicament in which she found herself, smiling back at a circle of dour faces. But she had a way with her. There were minor spits and sparks—she persisted in practicing her own religion in the midst of a populace that regarded the Mass as an abomination, and she distrusted and disliked her illegitimate half-brother, the Earl of Murray, one of the most powerful nobles of the land—but on the whole she got along swimmingly at first.

As the English, so the Scots. A queen must have a husband. The Hamiltons put forward their odd heir, Arran, the same whom Elizabeth had surreptitiously viewed and scorned. Mary too scorned him, but not surreptitiously: she permitted her scornfulness to show, a sight the Hamiltons didn't like.

The Queens dear-sistered each other in many letters,

all sunshine. At Elizabeth's suggestion they agreed to meet, and each started to plan what she would wear. This meeting, which would have been in the north of England, was several times postponed, and at last the idea was quietly dropped. Elizabeth's ministers were opposed to it, pointing out that Mary had not yet ratified the Treaty of Edinburgh, that she was not to be trusted, that her presence in the northern English counties might be a signal for Catholic revolt. It was not a question of the mouse hesitating to venture into the lion's den, but rather the other way round.

Elizabeth was humanly curious concerning the appearance of her cousin. When it was learned that one of Mary's suavest courtiers, Sir James Melville, was in London, she had him out to Hampton Court. Wolsey-built Hampton, convenient to London, yet in the country, on the river too, was one of her favorite palaces, as it had been her father's favorite, and she was wont to shine there. Melville neglects to tell us in his memoirs how she was dressed, but it is safe to assume that she glittered. She was thirty then, Mary was nineteen. Now, the Queen of England could be stately enough when an occasion called for it, but she preferred informal talks, little walks out of earshot of the court. Often she led a favored one aside, while hundreds of eyes followed them, trying to read their lips, the expressions on their faces. It was thus that she treated Melville when she pumped him about his mistress. Which of them was the better-looking? The soul of tact, Melville declared that the honors were even. Elizabeth danced for him: she was always eager to show off her dancing. There! Queen Mary also, Melville remarked, was an extremely graceful dancer. But could Mary play the virginals?

Very well indeed, Melville replied, adding "for a queen." (He was to hear Elizabeth at the virginals, after which he admitted that here certainly she was superior.) There were many other questions, adroitly evaded. Then came up the matter of height, a point upon which Elizabeth was known to be sensitive. "Is she higher than I?" Cornered, the Scot mumbled that in this respect Mary had the advantage, meaning that she was taller than Elizabeth. "No indeed, she hath not the advantage," Elizabeth shot back, *"for I myself am exactly the right height."*

Each of these women misjudged the other. Elizabeth could not bring herself to believe that Mary could move so swiftly and handle masses of men with such ease. In addition, when feeling most motherly, Elizabeth had a habit of writing little lectures, treating Mary like a child. The English crown had some sort of vague, unrecognized feudal overlordship over Scotland, or thought it had, by reason of the sundry Plantagenet invasions of old, and Elizabeth was wont to presume on this, a circumstance that didn't endear her to the Scottish nobles, still less to Mary. The "French woman," on her part, seriously underestimated her cousin of England, esteeming Elizabeth muddleheaded, as indeed by Mary's standards she was; but she also supposed that Elizabeth could be led around by the nose, and this was a mistake.

Elizabeth was inclined to be conciliatory, and said again and again that she would recognize Mary as her successor provided she herself, Elizabeth, did not have any issue, and provided also that the Treaty of Edinburgh was ratified. This Mary refused to do; but there was no harsh note in the refusal.

Arran had been turned down, but exalted circles south

of the border had other ideas. Why should not Mary marry an Englishman, so that her children, provided Elizabeth had none, might unite the crowns? The Duke of Norfolk was suggested. He was a Protestant, but politically he rather favored the Catholics. He would be acceptable to most Englishmen of whatever faith, a point Elizabeth insisted on. He had a wife, true, his third; but she wasn't well. Mary hesitated, or affected to. Somebody mentioned Lord Darnley. Then Elizabeth put her foot down, for Darnley was some more of Aunt Margaret's doing. Margaret Tudor, after the death of her royal Stuart husband, had married twice more, and by her second husband, the Scottish Earl of Angus, had produced the female who was now Countess of Lennox. The Lennoxes, deadly enemies of the Hamiltons, just now were in exile in England, together with their handsome son, Lord Darnley. The Countess, a scheming mother if ever there was one, had gone out of her way to snub young Princess Elizabeth at the time of the Wyatt business, but there is no reason to believe that Elizabeth bore her a grudge. Nevertheless Elizabeth refused a passport to the Earl and his son, who sought to return to Scotland for the ostensible purpose of restoring their estates. She could see what Mary was getting at. Darnley had royal blood in his veins. He was a Catholic among Catholics. In addition he was weak and a wastrel, though only eighteen.

At last Mary agreed, possibly with some mental reservation, to marry any English nobleman Elizabeth put forward; and it seemed that union was in sight. Maitland of Lethington, "the Scottish Cecil," came to London to make arrangements. He supposed that the senior queen, who was in a high good humor, would hand him a list of three or four highly placed possibilities, permitting her "dear sister" to make the final choice.

But Elizabeth had only one nominee—Robert Dudley.

We can't know, at this distance, whether she was serious. It may have been a calculated insult. Dudley was not only master of Elizabeth's horse but of her heart as well, and it was the common talk that they slept together. Yet Elizabeth persisted. She created Dudley Earl of Leicester. She even hinted that she might make him a duke. Dudley politely protested that he was "not worthy to wipe her [Mary's] shoes," in which of course he was right. The idea that she might have offended her dear sister did not *appear* to enter Elizabeth's mind. Ignoring Maitland's reluctance to discuss the offer, Elizabeth renewed it. In a nostalgic mood, she said that Robin Dudley was the handsomest and finest man in her kingdom, and she thought that she was doing Mary a great favor. She only wished that she could marry him herself, she said, but her subjects would not stand for that. She wished that Robin's older brother, the Earl of Warwick, had Robin's looks: then each Queen might have one, a cozy prospect. Maitland swallowed his astonishment and managed to reply that as Mary was so much younger, perhaps Elizabeth could marry Robert Dudley and have children by him, and *then*, when she had died, Mary could marry him—and thus they'd both have him. Elizabeth nodded thoughtfully, but made no reply.

In an unguarded moment soon afterward, perhaps dreaming of that brother-sister combination, that double wedding, Elizabeth let Darnley go. Mary pounced upon the "long lad" and, with the practiced air of a snake working on its favorite rabbit, fascinated him. Soon they were asking the Pope for a dispensation to marry, necessary because of their cousinship. Elizabeth, alarmed, broke into angry objections. But before the dispensation could arrive, Mary married the man anyway.

To call Darnley a disappointment would be to understate. He was a disaster. Had he been content to remain merely decorative, all might have been well, but he demanded the crown matrimonial, which would have given him power and rank equal to Mary's. He cried aloud for this, and stamped his foot. This spoiled brat, this mama's boy, was mixed up in a tough crowd now, and he didn't seem to know it. He was unspeakably proud, ostentatiously Catholic, preposterously pettish, and a drunk to boot. It got so that nobody paid him much mind; but when he thumped the table and screeched that the child his wife had been carrying these past five months wasn't his, *then* he got attention.

Laying a violent hand upon the monarch was high treason. Several years earlier a love-stricken youth had made an indecent proposal to Mary—physically, that is, so that she had to scream. *That* miscreant was drawn and quartered. Mary could hardly have cared for him, scarcely even knew his name. She did care for "Davey" Rizzio.

He was about thirty, and presumably handsome: we have no portrait. An Italian, he had come to Scotland in the suite of the Ambassador of Savoy as a professional musician. He stayed to serve the Queen, who must have found him refreshing after the vinegar-visaged Presbyterians. Mary always loved music, and Rizzio had a talent too for intrigue. Of course he was resented, and when he began to grow rich and put on airs, it seemed time to do something about it. Rizzio probably would have been cut down in the routine way, clubbed to death in some dark corridor perhaps, had not Darnley forced the issue by naming him as his wife's lover.

Darnley offered no proofs. We know today that the child Mary eventually bore, the future James I of England, had as many Lennox as Stuart characteristics, and had nothing Italian about him. They could not know that then. They didn't like Rizzio anyway.

They were not neat about it. They dragged him, screaming, out of the very presence of the Queen, stabbed him sixty times, stripped his clothes off, and pitched him downstairs.

Four months later the Queen was delivered of a male child. Elizabeth was said to have received the news while dancing, and to have sat down suddenly, a tragic, aging figure: "The Queen of Scots is the lighter for a boy, and I am but of barren stock!" It could have happened. Yet there was no reason for her to be surprised. Like everybody else in the civilized world, she had known about the pregnancy all along. She even had her christening present ready, a magnificent one, a gold baptismal font. This arrived too late to be used in the ceremony, but Elizabeth sent along a cheery note saying that perhaps it would come in handy *next* time. The font was later melted down in order to get money to pay the troops guarding the palace.

Mary was not a forgiving woman. It was Darnley's turn next. He met his end in a curious little two-story structure located just inside the old city walls of Edinburgh, not palace property, no longer church property, a sort of no man's land; and once again the job was bungled.

Darnley had been more than ordinarily tiresome. He

had fulfilled his function; having sired a male child, he was no longer needed. Surely he sensed this. Not only did he have no party, he had almost no friends. The Queen scarcely spoke to him. He began to talk wildly of running away and becoming a pirate. The Queen changed her tactics, waxing kind. Blue spots broke out on Darnley's face. Poison? A little later he came down with smallpox in Glasgow, and the Queen went to him; and when he had recovered sufficiently to be moved, or perhaps before that, she carried him, solicitously, by slow stages, back to Edinburgh, her own stronghold.

They were met outside the city by the Earl of Bothwell. Few historical villains are satisfactory in that role; Bothwell was. He had many weaknesses, but weakness was not one of them. He was big, he was bad, and, best of all, he was bold. He aimed at nothing less than the throne itself. Darnley stood in his way.

Darnley spent a week at Kirk-o'-Field, a building that was the old priests' quarters of a church now roofless and in ruins. A certain effort seems to have been made to shorten this time—perhaps several efforts. Lord Robert Stuart, one of James V's wild brood of bastards, Mary's half-brothers, seems to have picked a quarrel, and he was by blood a fit person to call Darnley out. There was talk of a duel, but no more than talk. Darnley preferred to stay in bed, or perhaps had to.

Mary meant to sleep at Kirk-o'-Field, she told Darnley in the presence of many, Sunday night, February 9, 1567. She was of course a very busy woman, but she would have spent that evening with her husband, she said, had she not suddenly remembered that she'd promised to appear at an affair. It was the kind of thing she could hardly get out of. Her favorite maid, Margaret Cawood, had been married that afternoon to one of the musicians, and the party was to celebrate this event. But she promised Darnley she'd be back early.

She had not yet returned at two o'clock when Kirk-o'-Field disappeared in an explosion.

Of the three men attending Darnley, one, asleep at the time, miraculously survived. Another was blown to bits. The third was found with his master forty feet away in the garden. These two were naked, and showed no burns or marks from the explosion. They had been strangled.

Public opinion then spoke, and its voice was unexpectedly loud. Darnley became a hero, a martyr. Nobody doubted—nobody does to this day—that Bothwell was the principal killer, the chief of the plot. Mary at first forbade a trial; and even when she submitted, the thing was a farce. The courtroom and the streets outside were packed with Bothwell retainers armed to the teeth. The crown did not even take the trouble to prosecute, in any proper sense of the word, and the acquittal, if it could be called that, satisfied no one.

All of this was bad enough; but now Mary lost her head. There is no other way to account for what happened. Two months after the death of Darnley her traveling party, a large one, was intercepted on the road to Linlithgow by a slightly larger one under Bothwell, and the Queen, it was more or less announced, was to be abducted. She spoke up quickly, asking that there be no bloodshed. There wasn't. Either that bodyguard consisted of the most chicken-hearted scamps Scotland had ever permitted to live or else it consisted of men who knew what was expected of them. Anyway, Mary was taken to Dunbar Castle, and there she was raped. That was her story—rape.

Three weeks later Bothwell's wife, a Gordon, got a divorce on the ground of infidelity not with Mary but with a slightly previous woman, a serving wench; whereupon Mary, protesting that she had to do this because she was pregnant again, married him.

Now, the kidnapping of royal persons, whether infant or adult, and the forcing of heiresses in order to get a claim on their inheritance—by Scottish law a marriage is not legal until it has been consummated—had been practiced many times, and would be practiced again, especially in the rough-and-tumble highlands. Also, highly educated, sensitive ladies like Mary Stuart, who was sometimes careless but never coarse, again and again through the ages have made fools of themselves over brutal, beastly, muscular men like Bothwell, and doubtless will continue to do so. Nevertheless, this was too much. Scotland rose. After his wife and Queen had solemnly commanded him to do so (for to give the man credit, he would have preferred to go down fighting), Bothwell skipped to Denmark, where eventually he was to die in a dungeon. Mary, head high, was led through street crowds that shouted "Burn the whore" and taken to Lochleven, a castle on an island in a lake far from the dangerous highlands, far, too, from any center of Catholic sympathy. There she was locked up; and for a little while Scotland was, for Scotland, quiet.

XIV

THE PHRASE "maritime enterprise," so often used in connection with Elizabeth's reign, could scarcely have been applied to early Tudor days, even early Elizabethan days, when England from a maritime point of view was one of the least enterprising of all nations. There were then a great many craft in the channel-crossing trade, though even these were more likely to be Dutch or French, in proportion to population, than English; there were a few warships; there were pirates; and —by far the greatest number of all—there were the fishing vessels. The pirates were small-timers, the Navy men part-timers. The channelers, from the very nature of their trade, were mariners of limited scope. Even the fishermen, who ventured farther to sea and did more actual sailing than all the others put together, went to the same places year after year. Nobody in England in those days envisioned any far horizons or gave a hoot that the world had recently been quadrupled. A Cabot, a Gilbert, was a crank.

A change was coming over all this, but it was not a sudden change. It started with the fishermen. When Henry VIII broke with Rome, the diet of the English people remained much the same, for few persons dreamed that the break would be permanent. As the religious laws were made more strict under Edward, however, and when Mary failed to win the country back to the Roman fold, Englishmen began to realize that they had never liked fish anyway. Capon, quail, goose, duck, fallow deer, red deer, mutton, beef: *there's* food. The rest, vegetables, fruit, bread, cheese, eggs, all that was then called "white meat," was useful only as a filler when there wasn't enough real meat, "red meat," to go around. Fish fell into that category. Fish was for poor folks, also for Fridays and holy days. But if you happened to be one of the new religion, Friday was the same as any other day, while there weren't any holy days at all. It is not suggested that anybody ever chucked the faith of his fathers merely because of a distaste for sea food; but once the change *had* been made, for whatever reasons, the proselyte took gleeful advantage of his escape from restriction. The fishing trade fell off. Thousands who, like their fathers and grandfathers, had never known any other work now had nothing to do. They were of course seafaring men, but even if they had wished to do so, they couldn't go far inland in search of employment, for the laws against vagabondage were almost unbelievably strict and cruel. There was no enlisting in the Royal Navy unless and until there happened to be another international crisis, and you would be discharged, probably without pay, as soon as that crisis had passed. In the circumstances it was no more than natural that they should become smugglers or pirates, or both.

The question of which was the cause, which the effect, need not detain us; but it is remarkable that there seemed to be an affinity between Protestantism and the sea. It was in the large cities, and especially in the seaports, that the new religion spread. It *paid* to be a Protestant, Catholics sneered. A Papist's ship or his goods at sea always were thought fair game. The pirates when they took a vessel would topple crucifixes, smash the images of saints, whuff out candles; and so it was that the Spanish, Portuguese, and Catholic French fell to thinking that all Atlantic pirates were heretics—and all heretics pirates.

It worked the same way with the French and Dutch. The celebrated "Beggars of the Sea" almost to a man were Lutheran or Calvinist. Virtually all the French pirates were Huguenots, and, like the Beggars, they often used English harbors as places of refuge, or for refitting, or as marts in which to sell their plunder. Time after time complaints were made by Spain and France to Elizabeth, who time after time said she knew nothing about it.

It must not be supposed that these pirates were picturesque persons with bepatched eyes, rings in their ears, bandanas wrapped around their heads, daring-staring fellows who swaggered, giving forth exotic oaths. No such thing. They were low, mean men, for the most part, who never got far from home. This was especially true of the English. The Dutch and French, who after all were rebels and could not always return when they felt like it, sometimes made longish voyages and occasionally combined to tackle a large enterprise—large as piracy went in those days, in those waters. The English were shore-based carrion. They swept up stragglers. The distressed, the half-wrecked, were their prizes. It was a dark and dirty business, and it gave England a bad name among nations.

True enough, Elizabeth couldn't ever have stamped out piracy, an ancient business that in certain bays and creeks was even an inherited right. It is equally true that she did not really try. Now and then the word was passed out quietly that it might be better to rest for a little while. But it was never for *longer* than a little while. For the rest, Elizabeth became an ostrich, saying from under the sand that there was nobody in sight at all.

All the same, it was these same greasy rascals, these offshore buzzards, who dumped into Elizabeth's lap some four million crowns, one of the greatest treasures the world had known.

It is necessary to go back a bit. The Habsburgs, who used to shuffle and spread marriage alliances with the dexterity of a prestidigitator manipulating cards, had emerged from the Middle Ages with a great deal of real estate, including Holland, Zeeland, Flanders, Brabant, and certain adjacent lands, known collectively as the Low Countries. When the empire was split in half at the abdication of Charles V, these Low Countries were put into the portion left to Philip II, King of Spain. The notion of a Spanish dominion over any country so remote from Spain, geographically, economically, culturally, linguistically, and so well developed in its own right, seems fantastic today. It didn't seem so to the Dutch and Flemings of the sixteenth century, eminently sensible folks who saw that they could not hope to survive without a certain amount of prearranged kowtowing to *some* great power. If it wasn't Spain it would be France, and of the two evils the Low Countrymen chose the one already at hand.

Now, these Low Countries were not a nation but seventeen provinces stippled with ninety-odd walled independent towns, besides many villages. The inhabitants had certain rights, affirmed by Charles V, and they were extremely stubborn about these. They submitted to heavy taxation on the part of the overlord of the fabled Indies, while they themselves made money hand over fist. They did not submit to the laws of religious uniformity. The upper classes, as in England, looked with a jaundiced eye on all change, religious or otherwise, being, above everything, intent on holding their own. Not so the rank and file. The Reformation found real roots in the Low Countries, where increasing thousands openly and earnestly worshipped as they pleased.

It was unthinkable to any prince or statesman that two religions could exist side by side. Charles V had watched with a sad heart the spread of the sinful Genevan flouting of laws by his Dutch and Flemish children, but he'd been too busy during his lifetime to cut out the cancer: he left this job to Philip.

The Act of Uniformity in England was not enforced either, at first. Elizabeth never did care what a subject's private beliefs were, so long as he went to Church of England services on Sunday. Lip homage was all she asked. It was in the first part of her reign that this moderation was most marked; and if the Catholics were, understandably, uneasy, at least they were free to do much as they pleased except in the matter of open profession. To Elizabeth there was no theological dispute. *She* was the head of the only church allowed, that's all. To have two different churches in the same kingdom would certainly be untidy and would probably be unsafe. But not until the Counter Reformation was well under way, not until the Catholics had begun to fight back and the country was being inundated with Jesuits and other such fiery and salamandrine spirits, did Elizabeth begin, a little by a little, to apply the laws Parliament had long ago passed.

Such moderation must have showed itself to the unimaginative Philip as nothing less than lunacy. Someday he would simply have to take over that island and run it right. Meanwhile he had the Low Countries, hotbeds of heresy.

Philip was always slow, but he was wondrously thorough. The very month in which the Scottish lords clapped Mary into Lochleven, June 1567, the Duke of Alva left Italy at the head of a magnificently equipped army, ten thousand tried fighting men accompanied by two thousand registered whores.

We have met this Alva as the proxy for his master when Philip was wedded to Elizabeth of Valois in Paris, where Henri II tilted once too often. A grim, sardonic man, he was at sixty the best soldier in Europe. He had this business well organized. Within three months of his arrival in the Low Countries he had caused to be hanged, beheaded, disemboweled, torn apart by horses, burned at the stake, or otherwise fatally injured, some eighteen hundred persons. This was in addition to many other punishments, notably fines. In the matter of fines, however, the Duke was disappointed. He had planned to pay his troops largely out of the money taken in; but the pigheaded Dutch had buried their coins, and seldom could the most prolonged torture wring from them the secret of the hiding-place. Paying soldiers for their services was still something new in Europe—until lately soldiers had been serfs called out by barons, counts, earls, or dukes, men to whom fighting a battle now and then was as much part of the conditions of their existence as tilling fields or milking cows—and possibly for this reason no system had been worked out. Habitually soldiers got their pay late, when they got it at all. It was their custom to make up this deficit with loot. But in the Low Countries there was no loot worth mentioning. Everybody knew that the burghers were outrageously rich; but they must have buried their plate with their coins, and once again the fools refused to talk.

This was too much for the soldiers. Though crack troops and under the severest sort of discipline, they began to mutiny. In the Low Countries, where each town was a separate unit, each garrison virtually an independent command, such a revolt was particularly hard to check. The best way to stop it would be to pay, and Alva had already sent a hasty begging letter to Philip, who, for once moving fast, had raised an immense sum, at ruinous interest. This was sent by sea, from Genoa, in six or seven ships. Why not by land? Because the gold and silver weighed so much that horses and carts for it, even if such could be obtained, would have been incalculably expensive. The condition of the roads was such that a caravan of that sort would take longer than ships, though obliged to cover only about a third of the distance. Moreover France, embroiled in a civil war, each side of which desperately needed money, was a good place to keep away from. So the treasure was sent by sea.

Why it was not given an escort is less clear. The pirates got after it, dozens of them, swarming like bees, off the south of England. The Italian seamen, fearing for their lives, made for Falmouth, Southampton, Plymouth.

Elizabeth was urged to seize them, but she lacked the nerve. Such a seizure would be an out-and-out declaration of war. Philip, a formidable antagonist at any time, just then had Alva's unbeatable army right across the Channel. England had no army at all.

Still, four million crowns was a lot of money. She decided that she had better have it unloaded and carried to the Tower of London, just for safekeeping: she wouldn't put it past those pirates to cut the treasure ships right out of an English harbor.

There was a prompt official protest.

This was how matters stood when Francis Drake came home.

XV

THIS lad Drake had already gone a-Guineaing. The phrase was new then, as was the racket. A few years earlier John Hawkins, scorning the local pickings, had sailed to the Guinea coast of Africa, kidnapped some Negroes, and taken them to the West Indies to sell. Philip II had decreed against the importation of slaves into Spanish America, a trade he earnestly wished to nip in the bud; for that matter, there were also laws forbidding colonists to deal commercially with any non-Spaniard. Hawkins knew this, but acted as if he didn't. The settlements he visited were small places, without garrisons, not fortified, for nobody until now had thought to challenge Spain's right to the Americas. Hawkins had only to train his guns on a given town and set a time limit to the negotiations. He contended afterward that the colonists *asked* him to browbeat them. Soon he had got rid of every black at a thumping profit, taking his pay in goods. So sure was Hawkins that Spain didn't mean what she said that he sent two of his vessels to a Spanish port, where they were immediately seized. Hawkins set up a howl. The line between piracy and legal reprisal was a thin one, when it was visible at all, and, Hawkins having proved that he could make money, it was officially decided that he had a claim against Spain —if he could collect it. He could, and did. His second voyage was like the first but on a larger scale, and this time he did not send any ships to Spain. The investors were well paid. One of them, Queen Elizabeth, made sixty per cent on her money.

Hawkins had founded the slave trade. He was made much of, was knighted, was granted arms with a chained "demi-Moor" (Negro) as a crest. The country was behind him. All trade must be free; and if from time to time the foreigners think that they don't need to buy or sell certain goods, then they should jolly well be *made* to.

Philip's course was clear. He had protested through ambassadorial channels, but this did no good: ostrich Elizabeth had her head in the sand again. Philip took sterner steps. When Hawkins sailed for the third time, he was a national institution. He did well for a while, and when at last weather and lack of supplies forced him to put in at San Juan de Ulloa (today's Veracruz), his vessels were so overloaded with loot that they would hardly float. It was here that the warships caught up to him. Hawkins fought hard and he did well to come out of it with most of his men and two of his ships, small ones, one the *Judith*, in command of his cousin, twenty-two-year-old Frank Drake. The rest, by far the greater part of the venture, was lost. The two vessels were overcrowded on the run home, and the men suffered woefully. Vague rumors of disaster had preceded them. Everybody knew that something terrible had happened over on the other side of the world, but nobody knew just what.

The *Judith* reached Plymouth first, right in the middle of the treasure-ship business. Its arrival could not have been better timed if young Captain Drake had been in the wings waiting for his cue. He was hustled off to London, where he told the story to horrified ministers, a horrified Queen.

Drake had a flair for homecomings; but though he was to make more sensational ones, he was never to make one of greater moment to England. The two events are not directly connected by any proof on paper, but there is no room for doubt that the tale of dark treachery at San Juan de Ulloa tipped the scales for Elizabeth and gave her the courage to clap the Spanish coins into the Tower.

Whether in the ordinary course of events she would have gone further in the matter we shall never know. Probably not. Most of her positive actions were taken in fits and starts—one step forward, three steps back—and it was up to her ministers to push hard when she was surcharged with confidence, to tut-tut and pooh-pooh when she quailed, thus inching the cause ahead.

In the matter of the four million crowns, however, it was the Spanish Ambassador who caused her to change her mind.

The first Spanish Ambassador of Elizabeth's reign had been a holdover from the time of Mary, de Feria, who was soon succeeded by wily, witty old Bishop de Quadra. The Bishop died in harness, all bebarnacled with plots, and in June 1564 Don Diego de Silva arrived to present his credentials. Fortunately for historians, he too was a writer of voluminous and extremely intelligent letters.

Now de Silva had retired, and Don Gerau de Spies had come. He was a Catalan. He did not know Elizabeth, and didn't understand, or could not believe if he had been told, that her first answer to anything was sure to be a long way from her last, that she had a passion for trial balloons. De Spies made a routine protest when Elizabeth took over the treasure, and she answered, naturally, that she hadn't seized it: she had only placed a guard over it as a favor to her dear brother of Spain. This was the answer that might have been expected; any other ruler would have made it, thus winning a little time. De Spies took it seriously. She was splitting hairs, and how was he to know that this was her usual practice? He supposed that she was defying his master. A hothead, he wrote to Alva recommending that all English ships in the Low Country ports be seized. Alva, not being in possession of the details, and supposing, mistakenly, that de Spies knew his business, complied.

That gave Elizabeth her chance. She proclaimed to the world, with a fairly clear conscience and even with a modicum of justice, that she had been grievously wronged. She had only been trying to help, and for this effort she had been punished by a rash, precipitate, and wholly unjustified seizure. The least she could do in retaliation was seize all Dutch, Flemish, and Spanish shipping and goods in England. Alva's smoking sword had sent thousands scurrying across the Channel, ships, goods, and all; so the value of what Elizabeth grabbed was four or five times what Alva had got.

Also, Elizabeth still had the treasure.

She had been looking into this, and she'd made an interesting discovery. The money did not actually belong to Spain. Spain had borrowed it, yes, but by the terms of the transaction, ownership rested in the lenders, various Italian bankers, until the treasure had been put ashore and turned over to the accredited representatives of the Duke of Alva. Therefore Philip II could not possibly use this treasure, which he did not own, as a *casus belli*. This was crystal-clear to the Queen, who added that she thought she might get in touch with the actual owners, the bankers. She could use a loan herself, she said. She did not add, didn't have to, that such negotiations were sure to take a long time—months, even years. Time was what she sought.

Elizabeth, then, had just done the most "Elizabethan" thing of her life so far, and she was breathless. As for the nation, it gasped—and with good reason. There was a near-panic.

When Philip II's third wife, Elizabeth of Valois, died, he promptly married again, the bride being his cousin Anne of Austria. The deed was done by proxy. The new Queen was to be taken to the Low Countries and from there by sea to Spain. The naval preparations this entailed, so near to England, were elaborate, and it was no more than natural that they should trouble Englishmen, especially just at this time. Was it possible that any one woman would rate so many ships? Was it not more likely that these were meant for an invasion? Philip had never had a better army so near, and certainly he'd never before been given so good an excuse. The English fleet, such as it was, was ordered to stand by. Fortifications were strengthened. The trained bands were called out.

It helped not a whit when, Elizabeth at last having consented to receive a commissioner to treat about the treasure, this commissioner turned out to be—not a moneyman, but Chapin Vitelli, a military expert.

Ambassadors then, like ambassadors now, though they were relatively more important, were of two kinds, regular and special. A regular ambassador was a very exalted personage indeed, and a special ambassador was even more so. Fifty would be a small suite for either; 350 to 400 was not unknown. Today, when diplomacy has degenerated to name-calling, it is interesting to see how our crude, semi-barbarous ancestors could shine at this particular sport. An ambassador going to a new place always had at least two, sometimes three or more, sets of instructions. Elizabeth was especially prone to this method of double-, triple-, even quadruple-dealing; more than one of her ambassadors, opening set after set of sealed orders, each of which contradicted the previous one, was made to look a fool. When Elizabeth could not dicker, squirm, sway away, return, shy off again—when she could not do this *personally*, as she loved to do, she did as much of it as she could by means of the written word. She was utterly cynical, but cheerful.

A special ambassador of course had a special mission, and it was easy to find a *fancy* special mission to cover the real one. Nobody was hoodwinked. You didn't need a staff of experts and the great chests of gold that no ambassador would travel without, in order to bestow the Garter on some monarch or perhaps to congratulate his wife on getting in the family way again.

Thus there was precedent for a military man being sent on a financier's errand, and the furor created by Vitelli's visit is a measure of the fright the English knew. Though he was armed with powers both extraordinary and plenipotentiary, his suite was largely stripped away in port. What's more, he was not permitted to stay long. What he reported to Alva we do not know. At any rate, the fleet that escorted the new Queen of Spain dropped sedately down the Channel without even getting near the English shore; and thousands who had been watching it exhaled in relief.

The treasure remained in the Tower.

XVI

THERE may have been some who believed or professed to believe that the Scottish lords had thrown into durance a crushed lily. The lords knew better. What they had in that bag was a wildcat, and they were afraid to let her out. At the same time, and though regicide was no novelty in Scotland, for political reasons they feared to kill her. France? No, France, where the Guises at the moment were in the shadow, showed only a formal interest in the captivity of its junior Dowager Queen. The loudest cries of indignation, the most insistent demands that Mary be set free, had emanated from, of all places, England. More, they'd been coming straight from Elizabeth herself.

If one hair of that woman's head was touched, she wrote fiercely, she would harry Scotland with fire and with sword.

To Elizabeth, a tremendous snob, a woman moreover who never was certain of the seat she sat on, the jailing of an anointed queen was sacrilege. She saw, or sensed, that the moral issue here was of the utmost importance, and that her own safety was involved. She said in no uncertain tones that Mary should be freed. She said it again and again.

The party in power in Scotland, perched precariously, favored an English rather than a French alliance. The outs, and especially the Hamiltons, pitched for the French, and Catholics, for Mary.

Mary's own half-brother, the Earl of Murray, now regent of Scotland, called on her at Lochleven. She was persuaded—by force?—to sign an abdication, also a proclamation of her baby as King. Mary hated Murray. She hated many another in Scotland now, and if ever she got out, heads would fall. They knew this. It is probable that they would have killed her had it not been for Elizabeth.

Elizabeth at this time surely did not think Mary guilty of any preknowledge of the murder of her husband, and though she must have been shaken by the "rape" and the subsequent sneaky marriage, she believed with all her heart that a royal person cannot be judged by ordinary human standards. A people might remonstrate; it never should revolt.

This was not the attitude of Mary's subjects, to whom there was nothing sacrosanct about a monarch. They for the most part never doubted that Mary was both adulteress and murderess, and, more to the point, a bad influence. Her Catholic supporters, in Scotland and England and abroad, had been shocked by the marriage to Bothwell, a Protestant. Elizabeth herself, it should be added, was by no means well liked in Scotland. Apparently unaware that she was hurting anybody's feelings, she persisted in treating her northern neighbors as though they were boys who had been bad. She was disgustingly closefisted. She was known to be immoral. More than once, too, she had proved unreliable. It had not been forgotten how she made great promises to Murray and his associates at the time of the pushing-out of the French, in order to get them to rise in arms—only to throw them over, after they had committed themselves, as soon as she got what she wanted. This piece of dishonest dealing—for such it was, though doubtless Elizabeth thought it shrewd statesmanship—was to come back and haunt her many a time in the course of her dealings with the Scots.

Just the same, a union of the crowns, even if it had to be on England's terms, was imperative, not merely advisable. The Scots may have gagged a bit as they swallowed their pride, but swallow it they did; while Elizabeth went on scolding.

At Lochleven Mary gave birth to stillborn twins, Bothwell's; but this did not mar her beauty or detract in any way from her charm. No matter where she was, Mary always found at least one young man—often there were a dozen—who yearned to risk his life for her. Ordinarily their heads did not need turning, a look at her being sufficient; but she had her wiles as well.

At Lochleven it was the laird's own son, young Douglas of Lochleven. It may be that a certain note of romance was added by the fact that his mother, a staid puritan now, once had been the mistress of James V, Mary's father. In any event, the young man fell head over heels in love, and when the condition was noted he was sent to the mainland. He returned—in a rowboat on a dark night. Mary had been ten months on Lochleven then. She borrowed a dress from a servant. All the storybook touches were there—the disguise, the muffled oarlocks, the horses saddled and ready, the young noblemen who dropped to their knees, tears in their eyes, to kiss her hand. And off she rode.

It was one of her most famous rides. She made Dumbarton, the Hamiltons' seat, that night. Her energy was amazing. Yet she was prepared to make concessions. The Hamiltons were not sending out the fiery cross simply because of loyalty. They had their price, the chief item of which was the marriage of Mary (as soon as she had divorced Bothwell) to Lord Arbroath, the Hamilton heir who had replaced Arran, now legally a lunatic. Mary consented. She would have contracted to wed Beelzebub himself if she thought it would help her to get back into power. Of course she repudiated the abdication.

There was a battle, not a notable one, at Langside, and the Hamiltons were routed. The Queen was hurried away, and once again her horsemanship saved her. Seven of them, including the infatuated young Douglas of Lochleven, rode cross-country, avoiding the roads, which were filled with the regent's cavalry, sleeping on the bare ground, eating what oatmeal and buttermilk they could beg, until on the third day they drew rein at Dundrennan Abbey to stare across a small stream, the Solway, at England.

This was Lord Herries's own land, and as an old border baron who knew every recess of that wild, lawless country, he assured her that he could keep her safe, if not comfortable, for more than a month. Meanwhile arrangements could be made to smuggle her back to France.

She shook her head. The borderers, rascals at best, had recently been given rough treatment by Murray, the regent, and they were not likely to risk a repeat performance. She might be betrayed, for there was sure to be a price on her head. She seems to have distrusted Herries too—mistakenly, for she never had a more loyal follower. If she skipped to France, it was likely that her mother-in-law, Madame la Serpente, after a sufficiency of ceremonial, would quietly clap her into a nunnery. It would be a very good nunnery, and very strong.

A woman of quick decisions, Mary called for a boat and crossed the Solway to England.

Elizabeth might have expected almost anything, but she had not expected this—a visit.

We would say today that she had a tiger by the tail. The Archbishop of York put it in a slightly different way when he wrote to a friend that Queen Elizabeth "had the wolf by the ears."

She just didn't know what to do. Eighteen years later she was still trying to make up her mind.

XVII

ELIZABETH was now in worse waters than she had ever known. Religion, with its tickle points of niceness, plagued her. On the one hand the Genevans croaked in doleful disapproval of almost everything—loyal men, trustworthy, but personally almost unbearable, while in politics they were given to some mighty touchy opinions. Soon she'd have a Parliament again, for she needed more money than the £200,000 a year the crown lands brought in, and the body would be predominantly puritanical, made up of stone-faces who would listen when she raged—and then do just what they planned to do anyway. Yet, though it must have pained her, she saw to it that the puritans got many of the strategic and lucrative places of power; it would have been folly to leave in the hands of Catholics the custodianship of royal castles, the stewardship of royal manors in the north, the wardenship of the marches.

On the other side were the Catholics, and what mischief were they up to?

Elizabeth tried to steer a zigzag course, skittering now right, now left. Or it could be that the tacking and veering was due, in part at least, to the vagaries of a mind by nature helter-skeltery. Those nearest to her dared not guess what she might do next, and this was particularly true in matters of religion. There were times when she seemed set on being shocking sheerly for the fun of it, so that spectators gasped as they wondered where it would all end: "This woman is possessed of a hundred thousand devils," de Quadra had written to Philip. At the beginning of her reign she seemed headed straight for Geneva, ostentatiously turning her back upon Rome. "Away with these torches, for we see very well," she cried when so greeted at a daytime ceremony of religious significance. She would heckle a preacher, interrupting his sermon. Yet she plumped for the fanciest vestments. Nothing was too nasty for her to say about married clergymen, and she would go out of her way to insult their wives.

She was not so profane as pictured. She had her dignity; and a woman who left three thousand frocks was not unaware of the importance of a good public appearance. On occasions when she referred to God with serious intent she made herself clear by dropping her voice, lowering her eyes: she generally referred to Him then as "the Creator." So we can't learn much, along these lines, from her language.

A person's private life usually is the key to his higher feelings and ideas; but Elizabeth didn't have any private life. She did indeed have a "private" chapel; but even it she used for either propaganda or perversity of mood, now mounting candles and a crucifix, now stripping it bare, one time having an altar, later a mere table, so that it was sometimes said, and not always in jest, that you could tell merely by peeping into the chapel whether Her Majesty today was going to prove Calvinistic or more Catholic than the Pope.

More and more she found herself pushed into the position of Protestant champion. This does not imply a reluctance to meddle in other people's business. All her life Elizabeth was offering to mediate: again and again she thrust herself forward with the suggestion that she be appointed arbitrator, and she always had on hand an oversupply of moral advice. Usually, however, it was not moral advice but money that was wanted.

Ireland, by reason of the refusal of the Irish to accept the new religion, was costing her almost a quarter of the annual income of the realm—with nothing to show for it. Scotland was in a state of near-anarchy and would probably get worse before it got better, if it ever did get better. The Huguenots just at this moment were not being expensive, but there was no telling when the position would change: they wailed that unless she married the Duke of Anjou, next in line for the French throne, their cause was lost, for the Guises would get back into power. The Low Countries looked the worst of all. It graveled Elizabeth to support or encourage any manner of rebellion against constituted authority. The Dutch, the Flemings were Philip's subjects, and there should be no earthly appeal for them from Philip's judgment. These were her true feelings. But a prince must be forever compromising, and if she didn't help the rebels, the French would.

Easily the greatest leader in the Low Countries was William of Orange, a prince, a Protestant. He is known to history as William the Silent, though Motley assures us that among friends he was garrulous enough, and it is certain that he never hesitated to ask for money. William did not coruscate, but neither did he ever fail to get up when he'd been knocked down. Like the later George Washington, if he was no great shakes as a soldier, he had something that in the position in which he found himself was far more important—faith in the future of his country. Soon, and almost in spite of herself, though only after a prodigious amount of haggling, Elizabeth was supplying him with money and also with those "volunteers" who were beginning to appear too in France.

She has been called fearless, but this assuredly she was not. It is not asserted that she quaked at the thought of bullet or poniard. Assassination was a possibility she had faced all her life, and just at this juncture it seemed all but certain. In Madrid no less a personage than Chapin Vitelli was vowing to do the job that following August in the country home of Lord Montague when Elizabeth paused there on progress; for various reasons this plan was put aside, but there were many other plots. Elizabeth's fears, however, were less physical, and had to do with her responsibilities. They had to do too with the Catholic Church.

She was afraid of that bull of excommunication some Pope was sure to issue. Elizabeth constituted a challenge to the unity of the Roman Catholic Church which could not be ignored. She had been lucky so far. Would the luck hold? How many of the seemingly acquiescent attenders of the Anglican service were attending only because they had to, and were secretly Catholic? For that matter, as she must have known, there were many thousands who were Catholic without taking the trouble to conceal it. The click of rosary beads was loud in the land; north of Trent, where the feudal system remained in force, where a Percy, a Neville, a Dacre meant more than any Tudor who ever lived, Mass still was celebrated openly.

It was the north that Elizabeth most feared—wild, poor country, more like Scotland than England, country in which a king or queen might be looked on as a foreigner. She had never gone there, never meant to.

Further, as an excommunication bull might be expected to be followed by a rising in the north, or perhaps all over the country, this in turn could well be the signal for a general rising of Catholics throughout Europe, a massacre of Protestants.

We know now that no such movement ever was officially afoot, though it was discussed. But the Protestants, enormously outnumbered and entertaining an inflated idea of the efficiency of the Church of Rome, stood aghast at their own temerity: they braced themselves, expecting at any moment to be squashed. They had of late been increasing, especially in France, but this could hardly continue. Their day would come. It was only a question of time.

Feeling this way, as hundreds of thousands of others did, Elizabeth was dismayed to have Mary Stuart cross the border. Her first impulse seems to have been to invite her dear sister up to London right away, to pay her all honor. She was soon talked out of that. Even as it was, in Carlisle, Mary was holding forth not at all like a frightened, trembling fugitive but rather like a conquering hero. People fought for a sight of her, a boon she did not withhold. From all directions the crowds trooped in.

For the north of England was Mary's own country. She had never before visited it, but she had been in correspondence with the principal nobles and gentlemen there for years, and she could be almost as seductive by post as in person. Here was the proper monarch both of Scotland *and* of England, in the eyes of all good Catholics. Even the Protestants conceded that Mary was next in line; while Elizabeth, far away in London, resolutely refused to do her duty and get married, as any decent queen should, so that the realm was at all times filled with the fear of civil war. But here was Mary, already equipped with a son, not to mention her heart-lifting smile, right in their midst.

She did not remain there long. Elizabeth had eyes to see. Mary was moved to Sheffield. She had comfortable quarters, plenty of servants, all the trappings of royalty, and repeated written assurances from Elizabeth that she would be restored to her throne as soon as she had cleared herself of those horrid murder charges. She was allowed to ride. She could receive visitors. The English crown provided funds for her maintenance, giving her the chance to use her own large private income on her party in Scotland. The English government refused to recognize her half-brother as regent or her son as King: it still referred officially to the Earl of Murray and *Prince* James. Just the same, she was moved—farther from Scotland, farther from the heart of the Catholic country.

A little later she was moved again, still farther away, to Tutbury—and barely in time; for the northern counties had risen in arms, while Michele Ghislieri, Pope Pius V (who was later to be made a saint), issued the Regnans in Excelsis bull, the bull of excommunication, stigmatizing "that servant of infamy, Elizabeth, who styles herself Queen of England" as "a heretic, and a fautor of heretics," freeing all her nobles, subjects, and peoples from any oath to her, and interdicting obedience to her "monitions, mandates, and laws."

It had come at last. Now the fight was in the open.

XVIII

EACH of these moves—the Rising in the North, the issuance of the papal bull—was a failure, largely because they did not synchronize. This remains a matter for amazement. Making all allowance for distance and the difficulties of communication, for divided command, weak leadership, Mary's condition of quasi-captivity, the jealousies and suspicion of the various European monarchs who were not getting on well with the Vatican just then, still the fact remains that the rebels rose first and were crushed, and months afterward the bull was published, giving off a low sodden *pop* like a firecracker with a defective fuse.

What would have happened had it been the other way round must remain one of the more fascinating if's in history.

The earls themselves, the plotters, were troubled as to whether they should wait for the publication of a bull. Their preparations were made, and you can't keep a thing quiet forever. Philip of Spain stayed remote, aloof, giving forth only an occasional consolatory word, perhaps a little money, no men. Alva in the Low Countries was skeptical: he would not move until the earls had shown that they meant business. They talked it over. Did they dare to disobey a queen to whom they had sworn allegiance unless they were relieved of this oath by the Vicar of God? Some priests averred that it was not necessary for the Pope to act, that the heretic had excommunicated herself when she refused a nuncio.

Others said no. The truth is, expert ecclesiastical advice was scarce in England just then. There were priests aplenty, and they went about pretty openly, but they were old-fashioned parish padres, men of no notable education, and certainly not up on the affairs of the great world. They were not the zealots who were soon to come piling in, in disguise, by every boat. Douai, Louvain, Reims, Rome had not yet disgorged the first of their graduates, dedicated young men of good family, men with a light in their eyes, a shout of exaltation in their throats. Here was another example of poor timing. With those steel-springed Jesuits to spur it on, the Rising in the North might have been much different.

Religion was not the only complaint. The Queen's refusal to marry had to be met. The two kingdoms could not be consolidated unless Elizabeth at least named a successor, or one was named for her—preferably, the northern noblemen thought, a Catholic, as a continuation of this insane anti-Rome policy might well mean war with either France or Spain. Mary, of course, was the one they had in mind. Yet they insisted throughout that their plot was not directed against Elizabeth in person. She was their Queen, and she had fallen into wicked hands, and what they were about to do would be done for her own benefit, really. This has a familiar ring; yet the northern earls were undoubtedly sincere. They were bitter about the "new men"—Dudley, Bacon, most especially Cecil—who were running things at court. It is hard today to realize that once upon a time a Cecil was esteemed an upstart, yet this is so.

These plotters, owners of vast lands, holders of great names, lords of many thousands, traditionally reactionary, resisted the new. They wanted the old-time respect for birth, for hereditary rights, and of course the old-time religion.

Despite a vibrant, taut straining of nerves, they might have waited a little longer had it not been for their leader. Norfolk, the head of the house of Howard, was the premier peer of the realm, its only duke. He was none too reliable a reed, but that any uprising could succeed without him was unthinkable. It was his own private ambition to marry Mary Queen of Scots—his third wife had recently died—and become King of Scotland, perhaps too of England. True, he was a Protestant, but not much of a Protestant; he was willing to be talked over, and so informed the Pope. He wavered, he drifted. He must have been shocked, this languid man, when he no more than contemplated a person as incisive as Mary of Scotland; and it is fair to assume that he found her treatment of past husbands disconcerting. There was no truth in it (it would have been a foolish thing for her to do, in the circumstances), but she was popularly supposed to have poisoned Francis II. Virtually everybody who was cognizant of the evidence, and this includes Norfolk himself, believed that she had a hand in the murder of Darnley. Her third husband, the ruffian Bothwell, she was about to disown. Yet the Duke, not hitherto thought a daring man, was willing to wed her. He permitted his name to be used. It was a great name, and it protected him for a while. Elizabeth would not lightly lay hands on a Howard. But Elizabeth did hear of his connection with the affair, and she did command him to come to London. After many excuses he started at last, but dallied on the way, once or twice all but turning back. Meanwhile the lords in the north were in anxious conference, wondering what they should do if he was clapped into the Tower.

Well, he was clapped into the Tower; and now the lords were afraid to move lest it cost their precious Duke his head. Soon Norfolk was released and permitted to go to his seat, which may have been sheer carelessness or may have been a master stroke of policy. We would say today that he was under house arrest; but with his hundreds of servants and retainers, and the mighty influence he wielded, he could easily have escaped and joined the dissidents. He didn't. Perhaps because they sought to force his hand, or possibly because they feared that he would be questioned further and tell even more than he already had, the lords of the north, not waiting any longer for that bull of excommunication (it was actually on the way), at last raised the standard of revolt.

It was not much of a rising. The earls of Westmoreland and of Northumberland were its leaders. Derby, cautious, stayed away. Norfolk too stuck to his seat. And Arundel. Sussex, whose loyalty Elizabeth most unjustly suspected because he was another great hater of "new men," not only refused to rebel but led the opposition.

The plan was to seize some good east-coast harbor and invite Alva to send his veterans; to dash for Mary (they never got within fifty miles of her, for she had been whisked away); to start in a most menacing manner for the capital in the expectation that the Queen would give herself up while the hated councilors fled abroad; and at all places to overthrow all signs of Protestantism, proclaiming a return of the ancient religion and the re-establishment of the Mass. The men behaved well. They were full of spirit, at first. A coast town was seized, though it was not held. The leaders were certain that the midlands and the south would rise in their support, something the midlands and the south utterly failed to do. Also, an army was being assembled.

It was not a very good army, not so good as theirs, nor so numerous; but Westmoreland and Northumberland decided to call the whole thing off. They escaped to Scotland, and their followers went home and tried to pretend that nothing had happened.

Indeed, not much had. Except for one disorderly engagement, more or less a military mistake, there had been no bloodshed. No foreigners had been brought in, no outrages committed. Mass had been celebrated here and there, but the skies had not fallen. The Queen and her advisors were untouched. Mary was safe under special guard at Tutbury. Yet the punishment was hideous, out of all proportion to the offense.

Elizabeth at first had not taken this rising seriously. Her one fear appeared to be that money would be wasted. Then her cousin Henry Carey wrote her from the field that Sussex was doing wonders with what he had but must have more if all was not to be lost. Elizabeth got busy at once, and at the same time she succumbed to fright. There is no other explanation. As it was not like Elizabeth to tut-tut what after all was a large-scale revolt against her rule, so it was not like her to bathe the battleground in blood. Yet there can be no question about the orders, which came right down from the top. Elizabeth may not have written them, but she certainly approved them.

No one who owned property was to be executed— not yet, for his property would go to his heirs. But if he was kept alive until a Parliament, called at last, could attaint him, *then* he could be hanged and the property would go to the crown. This was made clear to the captains in the field. Despite the absence of fighting, the affair had cost the throne much money, and Elizabeth meant to get this back.

On the other hand, the propertyless, a vast majority, should be hanged out of hand. Let there be plenty of examples.

She was obeyed. Guilt or innocence were not even inquired into; there was no sort of trial; men were simply selected at large from each village, on the assumption (close to true) that they were all guilty, and these were strung up—from trees rather than gallows, perhaps to save the price of timber. At least six hundred perished this way, their bodies left to dangle and turn, poisoning the village air for many weeks afterward, except where they were cut down, one by one, late at night by relatives.

This was not done while the heat of conflict still held. Yet neither was it done in cold blood, as a point of prepared policy, the way the Duke of Alva, for example, might have done it. Things like this were not uncommon in the Ireland of Elizabeth's day, where the English soldiery were greatly outnumbered; but that they should happen in England, and by direct command from the throne, caused a shudder.

Elizabeth was not a cruel woman. Her reluctance to order executions, especially for political crimes, more than once was the despair of her councilors. On this occasion she must have been very badly frightened indeed.

She was still in the grip of this panic when some

months later the Regnans in Excelsis bull was made public.

For some reason that eludes the modern student, the *publication* of such an instrument, rather than its mere *existence*, was what counted. Publication meant posting, as there were no periodicals. Elizabeth must have known of the existence of this bull, and how she could hope that it would remain unannounced passes all understanding. She might congratulate herself that so far it had caused no stir. France had done nothing about it. Philip had even protested against it. The Emperor Maximilian, no doubt thinking of his Protestant electors, had tried in vain to get Pius V to rescind the thing. It had been sent to Alva, who folded it and put it away.

On Corpus Christi day, May 25, 1570, a copy of this bull of excommunication was nailed to the door of the Bishop of London's palace in St. Paul's churchyard. It was of course quickly torn down. Not so quickly—it took several days—the man who had put it up was identified and arrested. He was John Felton, of London, a gentleman.

Now, the rack, that mechanically ingenious device of rollers and ropes used to pull a man slowly apart, was still an instrument of English justice: it was not abolished until 1628, long after Elizabeth was dead. Not often was it threatened, still less often used. There was a feeling of distaste for torture, which was resorted to only when certain highly placed personages believed that the safety of the realm demanded it.

John Felton was racked, and at what seems to have been undue length. For all his shrieks, his agony, and sweat, he could only say that there had been no plot, he'd done the deed on his own.

John Felton was tried, found guilty of high treason, and executed. The sentence used to read ". . . you must be hanged by the neck; but not till you are dead; for you must be cut down alive; and your bowels must be taken out and burnt before your face; then your head must be severed from your body; and your body must be divided into four quarters; and these must be at the Queen's disposal, and God Almighty be merciful to your soul." It was understood, however, that unless the executioner was uncommonly clumsy—the size of the crowd sometimes gave the fellow stage fright—the victim would be dead when cut down, thus cheating by a little the law that men were beginning to feel embarrassed about.

John Felton was still alive when he was taken down. The whole ghastly process was gone through with, and it wasn't hurried.

Only fear will cause such savagery. The Queen was afraid.

XIX

THE PARLIAMENT of 1566, in the form of a joint committee, kneeling, had begged her to marry. "I do not know what the devils want!" she had raged to the Spanish Ambassador, de Silva; but she knew. "She says that she is not so old that her death need be so perpetually dragged before her," de Silva wrote to Philip.

At the 1569 Parliament, called in order to get those lands cleared for the crown after the Rising, much the same scene was enacted. It made Elizabeth furious, but she thanked the committee, muttering promises that meant nothing.

Now she was going to have to call still another Parliament.

Elizabeth was the only Tudor who had trouble with Parliament. Individual petitioners or small groups she could fix with a scowl that caused men to tremble. She could even bully the court assembled. But faced with the organization of resolute men, she lost control of herself, alternately shrilling and trying to pour honey, to spread butter. She never concealed her dislike of Parliament. Previous Tudor monarchs had convened the body once a year. Elizabeth convened it only every third or fourth year when a financial emergency forced her to do so. She would greet it through an intermediary, customarily Sir Nicholas Bacon, the essayist's father. She would break in on its deliberations from time to time with a suggestion, disagreeably advanced, that the members stick to what they had been called together for and not go astray down dialectical bypaths. She'd sometimes jail a member whose speech offended her, later releasing him, taking her resentment out in harsh words hurled at a groveling committee of remonstrance, but nevertheless losing her point. Finally she would dissolve the Parliament as soon as she could, and as like as not she would do even this by means of a message that snarled.

Elizabeth was not normally an ill-natured woman. She had charm. It was not the charm of a *femme fatale*, as doubtless she liked to think. Still, for such as it was, she knew very well indeed how to use it. She could frighten, amuse, delight, all within a matter of minutes. She was marvelously well informed. Ambassadors who hated everything she stood for, and who had legitimate complaints for which they were given no satisfaction, returned from audiences chattering about her graciousness. What's more, she was easy to see, not standoffish. But though she could tread the labyrinthine path of diplomacy with a sure step, enjoying herself, when it came to doing day-by-day governmental business with an organized group of her countrymen she balked and swerved, spat and screamed, like some badly scared schoolgirl.

She had just about enough to run the country on *if* she could keep out of war. She had a monarch's customary revenue, from crown lands, tariffs, and the like, amounting to approximately £200,000 a year throughout the greater part of her reign, though toward the end it may have been as high as £300,000. She took her flyers—she was to make between £60,000 and £90,000 on a £3,000 investment in 1592 in the case of the captured Portuguese carrack *Madre de Dios*, the richest single haul on record at that time—but these could not be counted on. When war threatened, she had to look around for more money. Only Parliament could tax. Taxation then was the exception rather than the rule: it averaged scarcely £50,000 a year; and Elizabeth was forever trying to get along without it—that is, get along without Parliament—and forever failing.

The Parliament of 1571 she gravely adjured to "avoid long speeches," adding that it should not waste time over matters that did not concern it, such as the church, trade, the succession, foreign affairs. To this admonition the members paid no heed.

After the Rising in the North, Elizabeth had been petitioned by both Parliament and the Convocation, the bishops, to do something drastic about Mary Stuart. She refused.

The Mary affair was sadly complicated. Declining to meet her or to permit her to come to London until the matter of the Darnley murder had been cleared up, Elizabeth arranged for an extraordinary commission to hear some of the evidence. Mary, properly, refused to have anything to do with such a plan: she could be tried only by her peers, all of them presumably in heaven. It was explained to her that *she* wouldn't be tried. Her *accusers* would be tried. The Earl of Murray and his associates, the men who had forced Mary to abdicate and who now ruled for Mary's child, James, would in fact be the defendants. This fiction she accepted, perforce. No conviction was found. Much evidence had been withheld, and royal face more or less saved, but nothing was established, and the situation was exactly what it had been when Mary crossed the Solway, except that everybody was two years older now.

The question of what to do with her remained.

To deliver her across the border would be to sign her

death warrant. Mary was a vindictive person. Her half-brother and the other earls and barons who controlled Scotland, or at any rate controlled all but a few outstanding strongholds, surely could not afford to let such a person live.

To permit her to go to France might be to tip the balance of power there, giving the Guises a great gift, just when the Huguenots had been riding high. In Paris, in her own element, Mary might promote a return in force, which would mean French domination again and the open "postern gate."

To permit her to stay in England was to give all the dissidents a rallying point and invite further risings like the one just put down. Mary was not going to be quiet —there was not a docile bone in her body. Sent back to Sheffield, put again in charge of the Earl of Shrewsbury, a Catholic and an adherent of her cause, she rode, she hunted, she took the baths, at the same time keeping up an enormous correspondence. Become resigned? Mary would never become resigned to anything. You couldn't discourage the woman.

Whether or not there was any medical report to bear it out—probably there wasn't—the popular belief just at this time was that Elizabeth's death was near. (By this was meant a natural death: her murder was of course a daily possibility.) Mary on the other hand enjoyed exuberant health. Mary was the younger, she had a child. She was still marriageable. Almost all of Elizabeth's own ladies in waiting were in correspondence with her, as were many men of the court. A politician must look ahead.

There were two other possible steps.

Mary might be tried for her complicity in the Rising

in the North. This was what Parliament and the bishops urged. It was what Mary herself expected. *She* would never have shown mercy, in her eyes a sign of weakness. More arrogant than ever, she announced that when she left Sheffield it would be not only as Queen of Scots but also as Queen of England.

Finally there was assassination. The case seemed perfectly suited for it. Mary herself expected that an attempt would be made, and she was permitted to take elaborate precautions in the preparation of her food. After all, that was the way the game was played where she had been brought up. Assassination might not be polite, but a sensible prince had to think of his subjects, and of his own life too.

Elizabeth would not hear of it; and that was that.

Still she stood on a shaky platform, this daughter of Henry VIII. Whom could she trust? All around her, folks were muttering, glancing sideways. What she sought was merely peace. If she could just keep war away from England a little longer! But she was jostled, and she had nobody to protect her. Once again, then, she produced and flourished the most enticing of the prizes she had to offer—her virginity. Once again she put herself on the marriage market.

XX

CATHERINE DE' MEDICI had been married into the Valois family at fourteen, and for ten years she failed to produce an heir, so that her father-in-law, Francis I, was beginning to think of a divorce for her. That the Pope was Catherine's uncle would have made no difference—the Italians were a politically realistic people—but just then the lady started to do her duty; and, once away, she gave birth so briskly that by the time Montgomery's lance took the life of her husband she was the mother of nine. She was forty-four then.

Two only of the girls need detain us here. Elizabeth of Valois had been married off to Philip II and had lived a little in Madrid and had died. Margaret was about to wed Henri of Navarre.

The boys were four. The oldest, the first husband of Mary Queen of Scots, as Francis II ruled only a few months. The second was Charles IX, a small, misshapen creature who may have meant well. The third, Catherine's favorite, Henri, Duke of Anjou, was a sullen, darkly bigoted boy who wore rings on all his fingers, clanking bracelets and bangles as well, who painted his face, doused himself with perfume, and at private parties strutted in skirts. The fourth had been christened Hercules; but the preposterousness of this cognomen became apparent when he reached his full size, and the name was changed to François. Of Hercules more, much more, later.

It will be remembered that when Elizabeth's twitteration with the Archduke Charles of Austria had begun to assume serious proportions, Catherine de' Medici countered with a Charles of her own, the King of France. This resulted in a swirl of evasions, postponements, backtrackings. In time, disgusted, Lord Sussex withdrew as special ambassador to Vienna, cursing Dudley, whom he accused of conniving to get Elizabeth for himself. This was a blow to Cecil and others who, like Sussex, had honestly believed that their country needed the connection. Elizabeth was made to feel their disappointment. Perhaps she repented. Perhaps she broke loose for a little while from the spell of Dudley. It may be too that the Rising in the North had jarred her confidence in her own popularity. Whatever the reason, she broached the Habsburg marriage again. It was in vain. The Emperor said no. The Queen of England had made a fool of the Archduke Charles with those years-long negotiations, those multitudinous picayune objections. She must not expect Austria to be taken in like that again. When a little later the Archduke married a Bavarian princess, Elizabeth was hurt.

Charles IX of France too had married meanwhile. Like the Archduke, he could not wait forever. Yet the moment seemed propitious for an alliance with France, and Anjou was suggested. Another civil war had been ended, and by the terms of the treaty various exiles, Huguenots, were permitted to return. Two of the most distinguished of these, Chatillon and de Chartres, before they started back, broached the subject to Elizabeth, who said that she was too old to think of marriage but did not command that the subject be dropped. De Chartres and Chatillon had a purpose. It did not seem likely that Charles IX would have any children, and though young he was sickly, so Anjou might soon succeed to the throne. Now, Anjou was violent in his religious beliefs; his mother could not manipulate him as she did Charles, and if Anjou became King, the Catholic Guises might return to power. The Guise faction still banked on Mary Stuart, and proposed that Mary and Anjou be married secretly—by proxy, of course—and that Anjou then lead a French army into England or perhaps Scotland, gallantly release and embrace his bride (who also happened to be his sister-in-law), and thereafter with her rule both of the island kingdoms. Charles IX, hating his brother, was in favor of anything that would move Anjou from France. As for Catherine de' Medici, she sought a match between Anjou and Elizabeth for various reasons, at least one of which she shared with her sons—a curious one. She and they passionately believed that Philip had poisoned his third wife, Elizabeth of Valois. Why Philip should do that, after all the trouble and expense he had been to to make the match, they did not say; but that's what they believed. They hated Philip now—and the most effective way to hate Philip was to make up to Elizabeth of England.

It might seem, at a glance, that all signs pointed to this union. This was not so.

There was Anjou himself, just turned twenty, a discontented, unpredictable, fawned-upon fop, increasingly under the influence of the Guises, who were ready to move heaven and earth in order to prevent his marriage to the heretic Elizabeth. Anjou professed to be horrified by the thought of sleeping with a woman of thirty-nine, a woman he had been told had a crooked body.

There was the English public, which still inclined to the belief that the only good Frenchman was a dead Frenchman.

There was Elizabeth, who dearly loved marriage negotiations, loved them so much that she hated to see them terminated, even unsuccessfully. It was "all dalliance," Anjou grumped; but La Mothe Fénélon, the French Ambassador, egged on by Catherine, with rolling eyes vowed that the Duke of Anjou was a man among men. Elizabeth sighed and murmured that she was sought not for her person but for her possessions. La Mothe insisted that this was not so. Elizabeth said that the princes of the house of Valois were notorious for their infidelity. La Mothe protested that she was wrong about that, though on the spur of the moment he could not give an example of one who had been true; but after all, where was there a precedent? When had such beauty as Elizabeth's been known before? Elizabeth muttered that her beauty, alas, was faded. La Mothe called upon the heavens to look down and avouch that beauty such as hers could *never* fade.

This went on for weeks. The Frenchman began to believe that Elizabeth might mean at least a little of it. A lowering Anjou averred that he would never marry a woman of no virtue. Catherine de' Medici all but went out of her mind. That such a trifle should be thought of in connection with so magnificent a match! In time she and others talked Anjou out of his sulk, and a formal written proposal, bristling with qualifications, was sent to England. It was then that the serious conferences began. These were not wrecked until the Queen, presumably because she could think of no other objection, fell back on the stipulation that had stopped the Archduke—that no manner of Mass, not even a private ambassadorial one, should be permitted at any time in England.

She might have been less fussy. Affairs in Scotland were going badly for the English party. There was a rumor (it was false) that Alva was about to invade England, and another (this one was true) that Philip was making preparations to take over Ireland, where conditions from the English point of view could not possibly be worse. In every way indeed, all over Europe, the Spanish agents were doing whatever they could to block the proposed match.

XXI

SHE must have supposed that Philip's forbearance was inexhaustible. The slave trade was continued, shotted cannon insisting upon this. "No peace below the Line" had become the cry of English corsairs, who now were venturing far from home: Oxenham even had a peek at Philip's private ocean, the Pacific, and if he hadn't loitered to make love to a Spanish lady, he might not have been caught and hanged as a pirate. The news leaked out anyway. Drake had been given leave to recover his share of the loot lost at San Juan de Ulloa in any way he saw fit, and the way he saw fit was the seizure of every Spanish ship in sight and the storming and sacking of Nombre de Dios. The narrow seas swarmed with freebooters who sold their spoils in English ports. It was to these ports, again, that they ran when chased. Several Spanish war vessels, for example, drove the pirate Brederode, a Dutchman, right up under the cliffs of Dover, and they were about to close in to sink him when the shore batteries opened up on *them!* There were protests, of course, but there was no war.

Elizabeth was peeved in particular by the fact that so many English Catholics found refuge and even employment in the Low Countries. Books and pamphlets were printed there, and "bookrunning" became an accepted form of smuggling. At one time the Catholics had their own underground printing-press in London, which was moved from place to place and manned by persons in various disguises, and which never was raided; but in the long run it was found easier to smuggle the reading-matter in from Holland. What Elizabeth expected Philip to do with these refugees would be as hard to say as why she thought she had any cause for complaint while she herself was putting up thousands of Protestant refugees from the Low Countries.

She did have one legitimate grievance. When an English ship put in at a Spanish port, it was likely to be boarded by soldiers, who arrested all mariners and turned them over to the Holy Office—that is, the Inquisition. The best these men might expect was years in a noisome dungeon. Time after time Philip replied to protests by saying that he had no authority over the Holy Office. The stubborn English just didn't believe it.

Elizabeth sent a special ambassador to Madrid—it had been more than a year since England withdrew its regular ambassador—to protest these two points anew—the refugees in Flanders, the jailed sailors. Did she expect Cobham to be greeted with open arms? Spain needed England's friendship, but Spain had its pride. Cobham was received with heavy polysyllabic politeness; he was impeccably insulted; he was sent back.

At that, he fared better than Don Gerau de Spies, the Spanish Ambassador to England, who was mixed up in the Ridolfi plot.

Roberto Ridolfi di Pagnozzo was a Florentine banker who had lived in London for ten years. A secret agent of the Pope, he was a born go-between, a whisperer. The plot that bears his name was a classic, incredibly complicated, and by no means easy to crack. Cecil worked months on it, studying cipher messages, instructing *agents provocateurs*, listening to reports, spending a good deal of time too in that low-ceiled room in the

Tower where the ropes and rollers were. Today we know every detail; but it came hard then, and slowly.

Elizabeth was to be assassinated, Mary freed and crowned, Norfolk was to declare himself a Catholic and then get married to Mary, Alva was to cross the Channel with ten thousand troopers. The plot was well financed and, as such things went, well organized. It was also extremely well exposed, one of the most workmanlike jobs of counterespionage on record.

Ridolfi himself was on the Continent when the bubble burst. He had seen Alva, who would do his duty but didn't think much of this *"gran parlaquina."* Ridolfi was having better luck at the Vatican. Of course he never went back to England.

The Bishop of Ross, Mary's Ambassador in London, surely one of the slipperiest plotters of his time, was allowed to go free, a badly frightened man.

Don Gerau de Spies was haled before the privy council and told that he had three days in which to pack. On the way to the ship he made all sorts of excuses for delay, hoping to hear at any hour that the Queen had been killed. But this part of the plot too had been anticipated. When at last Don Gerau did depart in a cloud of threats, he had no glad tidings to take back to his master.

As for Mary, once again both bishops and Parliament petitioned Elizabeth to do away with that "bosom viper," and once again Elizabeth refused.

The first prisoner of all, a moonstruck young Mary-worshipper named Bailly, was tricked by a spy into revealing what he knew, and then was hanged. Many, many others were executed, the most distinguished of them being Norfolk. The House of Peers found him guilty January 16, 1572, but it was not until June 6 that his head came off. The interval had been spent in trying to persuade Elizabeth to sign the death warrant—and to *keep* it signed, for she had several times signed and then recalled it. It was hard to kill a Howard. Her father had never thought so, but she did.

Thus it was that Spain and England drifted further apart, despite all Philip could do.

Thus too, and by the same token, England and France got closer. The Anjou marriage negotiations had broken down, but Catherine de' Medici still had a son left, Hercules-called-François, the Duke of Alençon, physically the most repulsive of the lot. She offered him as a husband, whereupon Elizabeth murmured something about her age, and La Mothe Fénélon cried that no man ever had known such a ravishing bride, and Elizabeth sighed that the princes of the house of Valois were known for their wandering eye, causing Fénélon to call upon heaven to bring about his immediate disintegration if the Duke of Alençon was not in all truth a man among men, a nonpareil, handsome beyond description, and devoted to that fairest of womankind, that loveliest flower in the garden of femininity, that—

So everybody was happy again; and in that frame of mind they signed a treaty, the Treaty of Blois, April 19, 1572. Philip was in despair. In Paris, preparations to take over the Low Countries went ahead.

Unfortunately other things were happening in Paris at the same time.

Now Madame la Serpente got caught in her own toils. The civil war had ended. The Huguenots had laid down their arms, and this event was to be signalized by the marriage of their highest-born, Henri of Navarre, to Margaret, sister of the King. The ultra-Catholic party had opposed this match, but Catherine insisted on it, and the King himself, her puppet, had given it his blessing. Paris was crowded with Huguenots come to take part in the week-long celebration, and one of these, the greatest, their natural leader, was Admiral Coligny.

Had Catherine given these heretics too much rope? The Low Countries soon would fall to France. This seemed sure, with both sides in the late civil war joined. But wouldn't the Huguenots get too much credit for having brought it about?

There were seething masses of hatred, black and bitter as gall, fanatical hatred, bigotry of the beastliest kind, in the breasts of thousands of Parisians, a condition exacerbated by the presence of so many Huguenots. Catherine was not counting on these feelings. She may not even have known of them. What she did know was that Admiral Coligny appealed to her oldest son, the King, as the very epitome of wisdom. This she couldn't tolerate. She was no longer regent: Charles was of age now. She had no party of her own to fall back on. Her power lay in her influence over Charles IX, who until now, until he had got to know this man Coligny, had been putty in her hands.

Coligny must go. She took the matter up with the Guises, who were eager to come back. The wily woman seems to have had some plan for playing both ends against the middle, hoping that the leaders of each side would kill themselves off in another civil war—but a small war, a controlled war, right here in Paris. She had never been more wrong.

Coligny was shot from ambush. He lost a finger and his left elbow was smashed, but he was otherwise sound.

Charles IX was playing tennis when he got the news—playing with the Duke of Guise himself—and he slammed his racket down in rage. He visited the Admiral, Catherine and Anjou trailing him, fearful of what he might learn. He sent Coligny presents, put a guard around his house. He vowed that there would be a full investigation.

This looked dark indeed. The shot had been fired from a house belonging to the Guise family, and a man had been seen to flee from that place soon afterward, a professional bravo named Maurevel, on a horse identified as one from the Duke's own stables. The Guises would be questioned, surely, and they might tell who had put them up to the job—Madame la Serpente herself. She must strike.

Paris had the uneasy, jerky air of a man who keeps looking over his shoulder, afraid that he's being followed. Some of the Huguenot leaders were for clearing out, even at the risk of being called cowards, in order to avert a general uprising. Others said that to desert the Admiral, who couldn't be transported, would be to doom him to death. They stayed. Wild stories crackled and spat in the overcharged air. Everybody seemed to sense that something tremendous was about to happen.

The night of August 23 Catherine de' Medici, her second son, Anjou, so recently Elizabeth's reluctant suitor, and several others worked for an hour and a half over the poor weak-willed King. Catherine made no bones about the attempted murder. She had connived for it, she said, in order to save him, her son. The Huguenots planned to seize him and use him as a hostage, ruling France. They would strike at any hour now, any minute.

At last the King broke down. All right, kill the Admiral! he cried. Kill them all, every Huguenot in the country! And he flung out of the room.

They took him at his word. They had a little list. It contained fewer than a dozen names—or so they were to assert later. It was headed, of course, by that of Coligny.

The slaughter started at dawn. It had been planned with a hellish ingenuity, and it was carried out almost without a hitch—for the first few hours. There was no pretense of trial, no rustling of warrants. Known Huguenots, together with their wives, children, servants, simply were run through the body. There was no time for any sort of organized resistance. The victims were all in night clothes. In most cases the bodies were hauled out into the streets so that the mob could mutilate them, clubbing them, hacking off members for high exhibition.

This was bad enough; but about the middle of the morning the mob began to take over. Gone was efficiency, controlled ferocity. All was chaos. Even babies weren't spared, even household pets. Through that day, that night, and all the next day and next night, with no sort of break or intermission, the killings continued. Because of the summer rains the Seine was exceptionally high, and this was well, for otherwise it would have become clogged with bodies. The streets of Paris, the pavements, were literally awash with blood. The fury of the mob was such that mere death did not sate it. Dismemberment must follow. Each body was flayed and slashed and chopped in a maniacal manner.

Catherine and her little list! No exact figures are available, if only because most of the victims were visitors to Paris. The lowest estimate is two thousand, the highest ten thousand.

This was only the beginning. When word got out that Huguenots were being killed in Paris, there were massacres elsewhere—Orleans, Rouen, Toulon, Lyons, Bordeaux, Meaux, many other towns and cities—all of them spontaneous, all unspeakably savage. This went on for weeks. At least fifty thousand persons were killed.

It is not easy to imagine the dismay with which the first wild rumors of this madness were met in England— rumors to be followed immediately by those Huguenots lucky enough to escape, a swiftly increasing flood, every possible boat being pressed into service—but surely the average man must have said to himself, with a sudden sinking of the heart, a dry mouth: *This is it!* There was no panic, as there had been at lesser and less justified rumors of invasion, but the nation grimly prepared for war. This was what they had feared, the great Catholic uprising that was to sweep the civilized world. There could not be the slightest doubt, men said, that it would jump the Channel. *Here it comes! It's our turn next!* Swords were sharpened, gunpowder was hauled up from storage. The fleet was ordered out.

The matter was made even more horrible, and to Englishmen more menacing, by the attitude of the Vatican, where Gregory XIII ordered bonfires lighted, a medal struck.

One man at least was, if startled, pleasantly startled. It was said that Philip of Spain, when he heard the news, laughed for the first and only time in his life. Now he need worry no longer about that Anglo-French alliance.

Appalled, but only momentarily, Catherine de' Medici

concocted a story essentially the same as the one she had told the King. This action had not been a massacre at all, but the nipping-in-the-bud of a bloody and outrageous uprising. The very life of the King had depended on swift action. And so forth.

La Mothe Fénélon, eager to take this explanation to Elizabeth, asked for an audience. Now the Queen of England was a singularly accessible monarch, as monarchs went in those days. She could be ceremonious enough when the occasion demanded ceremony, and at any time she would poniard with a glance a courtier who went too far; but the day-by-day informality of her court, wherever it was located, was the talk of Europe. Moreover the French Ambassador at this time, an amusing fellow, was a particular pet of Elizabeth's. Yet she could put personal preferences aside, as a prince must. La Mothe was, after all, France. Three weeks passed before he was at last received, September 8. This was at Whitehall, the "official" palace. The audience chamber, an austere place, was draped in black. The courtiers all wore mourning; the Queen wore mourning.

The rebuke was well thought out, and had great dignity. La Mothe was received in icy silence, his explanation was heard without comment. The Queen then said the proper things properly, but said no more. When La Mothe ventured to bring up the courtship again, she cut him short. It was no time to be talking about marriage.

XXII

IT had seemed that Ireland could not get worse, yet Ireland did. Elaborate colonization schemes, which took into consideration just about everything except the Irish people themselves, failed. Humphrey Gilbert and young Devereux, the very soul of chivalry, broke their hearts and pocketbooks, not to mention many a skull, and still reports made doleful reading. Then the Desmonds rose. . . .

Scotland was in a state of near-anarchy, torn between the King's party and the Queen's. Murray, whom Elizabeth still refused to recognize as regent, generally did the right thing, but he did it in a dull, determined way: as Disraeli was to say of Gladstone, he was a man without one single redeeming vice. Not until a disgruntled Hamilton slew him from ambush did the people begin to see his high merits, and then, as is usual in these cases, it was too late.

The next regent, Lennox, also was slain—this in the course of an abortive attempt to kidnap the boy-king from Sterling. Soon afterward the doughtiest of them all, Morton, was hanged for his part (a trifling one) in the murder of Darnley. All of this Elizabeth found offensive, and it made her furious when anybody north of the border tended to distrust her, though her whole policy in Scotland had been one of lies, false promises, prevarication. Once, exasperated, she sent three well-organized bodies north of the border to harry an area twenty miles deep from sea to sea, leaving not a stone house unsmashed, not a hut unburned, nor any animal alive. A more enduring victory was scored when she sent a company of artillery to Edinburgh, where after eleven days of bombardment the Castle, hitherto impregnable, was surrendered. This was a high point, almost a turning point, in the history of siege operations; but immediately, and to the Queen, its interest lay in the fact that Edinburgh Castle had been the last fortified place holding out for Mary Stuart.

An additional irritant was the attitude of the young King, who, as he grew up, began to show signs of having ideas of his own. He was in correspondence with his mother now, and seemed to think that she had been harshly dealt with. In the various tentative treaties Elizabeth at this time was negotiating with Mary, setting forth the conditions under which she would live up to her promise of restoring Mary to her throne, there were some fantastic provisions. Elizabeth stipulated, for example, that hostages should be sent to London, that English garrisons should be stationed at Dumbarton and at Edinburgh, that Leith should be open to English warships, and she never failed to provide that the Prince (as she persisted in designating James) should be brought to England for education. Other nations had designs on young James. The Guises were laying plans to seduce him. Mary, his mother, though she still wrote her "dear sister" trying to get a personal interview on the plea that she had some stupendous secret which she could communicate only by word of mouth—Mary always believed that if she could get into Elizabeth's presence she could twist the older woman around her finger—at the same time was writing Philip advising him to invade England and as a beginner to kidnap Mary's son and bring him up in Spain.

From the Low Countries too came little but bad news. Commercial relations with England had been patched up, more or less. Alva had been recalled to Spain, where as Philip's chief advisor on Low Country affairs he urged again and again that Elizabeth be treated with great respect. This was good: and so was the circumstance that William of Orange, if nowhere victorious, at least had somehow kept the field. But the general picture was black. William kept calling for more men, more money. It went against Elizabeth's principles to support a rebellious subject against his master. Alva's successor Requeséns, had orders to try appeasement, reconciliation, but it was too late; the Dutch would never consent now to be ruled by Spain on any terms. The civil wars that had broken out in France again after the St. Bartholomew massacres were at the moment scarcely simmering; and this, good for humanity, was not good for Elizabeth. The French were in arms and looking for trouble. Specifically there was the Duke of Alençon: he was a fool, but he was still a Valois, and something had to be done about him. Charles IX had died, and had been succeeded by Anjou as Henri III—a young man who fancied female clothes and was not expected to have any children. Henri III was treating Alençon precisely as *his* brother had treated *him* when Charles IX was on the throne and he himself next-in-line—that is, he was willing to do almost anything to get the man out of the country. Alençon was unmarried, and the one next in line of succession to the throne was Henri of Navarre, a Protestant! Therefore Alençon could not be quietly done away with. On the other hand, he could not be allowed to linger in France, where his name and his prospects would make him a rallying point for rebels. An adventure into the Low Countries seemed called for. Alençon's religious convictions, if any, were pliable: he had even been a Protestant for a short while. If he lost, his life would probably be saved. If he won, he'd have a kingdom for himself.

The plans for the partition of the Low Countries were without number, and Elizabeth was included in each, but she fought shy of every effort to thrust additional sovereignty upon her. She had all she could do at home. This unimperialistic policy on the part of a person who has been hailed as the grandmother of British imperialism, if it served only to make other nations suspicious, certainly expressed Elizabeth's own beliefs. "It may be thought simplicity in me that all this time of my reign I have not sought to advance my territories, and enlarge my dominions; for opportunity hath served me to do it," she was to say on dissolving the Parliament of 1593, "and I must say, my mind was never to invade my neighbors, or usurp over any; I am contented to reign over mine own." At about this time, for instance, when the rebel fortunes looked uncommonly low, Louis of Nassau proposed in the name of his brother, William of Orange, that Flanders and Hainault go to France, Brabant and Gelderland and Luxembourg to Germany, Holland and Zeeland and the islands at the mouth of the Scheldt to England. Elizabeth said no. On more than one occasion, too, Elizabeth had been offered the overlordship of the whole place, and she refused even to consider it.

She was proud, as she had every right to be, of the way in which the religious problem had at first seemed to work out. She was, in this, the amazement of Europe. What had happened to the English Catholics? The bishops she had inherited had with a single exception resisted the change, preferring jail. As it happened, there had not been many bishops; a number of the sees were vacant, a stroke of luck for the new monarch. The priests, if by no means unanimous, at least had put up some show of recalcitrance. The communicants in general didn't seem to care. It is not possible that millions of persons were utterly cynical, willing to be flipped over, like so many pancakes, from the old belief to the new. Allowance must be made for the skill with which the reconversion was brought about; the need for clinging to the new monarch at least long enough to permit her to get established, lest the country be plunged into religious warfare; the superlative spying skill of Cecil and later of Walsingham; the lack of local leadership; most of all the easy, amiable, unpushing way in which the laws of uniformity were enforced, or rather *weren't* enforced. Still, "there is no getting away from the shame of that great defection," as one thoughtful Jesuit was to put it.

The truth is, the rank-and-file Catholics in England had been badly let down. They were bewildered. Should they take the oath to Elizabeth? The ones on the large feudal estates were given no choice: they were not supposed to think for themselves. But there were many others. There was nothing inherently disloyal about them: all they asked was to be told whether church or country should come first. There were still priests in the land, but they were worn-out men, as confused as their communicants, for they lacked all direct orders, all association with their ecclesiastical betters or even among themselves. The Catholics of England, for all the widely varying estimates of their numbers, and their lack of organization, comprised an extremely important piece on the chessboard of European politics. In a dozen capitals they were discussed, weighed, calculated. But nobody seemed to give a hoot for their individual souls. From where *they* stood, blinking, mouths agape, it must have seemed that the Church in Rome and the Holy Father had forgotten all about them.

Then a change came. Rome began to fight back. There was the Council of Trent—by no means all that had been hoped for, but nevertheless substantial, a statement. There was the excommunication bull, a dud in its immediate effect but still a *thing in being* which might yet be used; it was being proposed, for example, that Guise should lead a French force into England to free Mary and depose Elizabeth, and that he should do this *not as a Frenchman* but as a Catholic carrying out a Papal decree, thereby giving Spain no excuse to interfere. There was a general toughening of the Catholic attitude, with the understanding that the old, rotten, beautiful, decadent, gorgeous, bad days of the Renaissance Papacy were gone forever. Most significant, there was the realization that such Catholics as were left in England—nobody will ever know how many had dropped out—needed help.

Soon the young men began to come—priests, Jesuits most of them, English (or Scottish) to the bone, returning refugees carefully trained. They had been adjured to keep away from all talk of politics, but this was difficult to do, and in any case, simple assertion of the Pope's supremacy now constituted treason. Aside from her own humane tendencies, Elizabeth did not wish to make martyrs. But the challenge had to be taken up.

Spokesmen for Elizabeth always contend that in her reign no subject ever suffered torture or death, or even prolonged imprisonment, because of his religious beliefs. Those who were racked were racked only in order to get information about plots against the Queen; while those who were hanged (it had the same effect on their necks) were hanged not as Catholics but as traitors. There were none of the burnings that had besmudged Mary's reign. Estimates give Elizabeth 250 Catholic deaths (not counting the Rising in the North) in thirty years, as compared with 300 Protestant deaths in five years under Bloody Mary. It was bad enough. She did not like it.

Yet this and many other matters were laid aside when in 1578—it was spring, and perhaps that had something to do with it—the Duke of Alençon suddenly remembered the woman he had sought to marry some six years earlier, and wrote suggesting that they renew the negotiations. It threw her into a fit of excitement. She was forty-four, he twenty-three, and they were about to spend the next three years in the most farcical courtship on record.

XXIII

THIS time the preliminaries were brief, for Alençon was eager and Elizabeth had been shorn of many excuses for delay.

There were two precedents. The negotiations in advance of the Philip-Mary nuptials had resulted in an agreement almost exactly similar to that the commissioners who discussed the possible Anjou match fifteen years later were to frame. The Anjou negotiations had broken down when Elizabeth, almost as a last resort, stipulated that the Frenchman could have no private Mass in England; after which Alençon had been substituted for his older brother in negotiations that were broken off by the St. Bartholomew massacres. But Anjou, now Henri III, was a narrow-minded man. Not so Alençon. "I do not doubt . . . but that he would be reduced to any conformity," wrote a wry Walsingham.

Walsingham opposed the match, as did, in the beginning, virtually every other councilor worth mentioning excepting Sussex. They were jolted by the avidity with which their mistress took up the offer. They could only attribute this to one of her freakish fancies, and assume that it would soon pass. They took it for granted that when she had tired of playing her little game, or had perhaps hit whatever mark she was aiming at—*they* could see none—she would close the proceedings with her customary demand that the Prince appear in person. Alençon probably would not stir then; but if he did come, the councilors foretold a swift ending to the affair.

For this François de Valois was short, almost a dwarf. His face, extremely dark, was scarred with smallpox pits. His eyes popped, rolled. He had a nose so deeply cleft that it showed at first like two noses, bulbous, vinous, very fat. His legs were knobby. He bounced when he walked.

Elizabeth liked her men handsome.

Alençon sent an emissary, his master of the wardrobe, Jean de Simier. This little fellow arrived a month later than the time he was expected, and the Queen, who was giving every sign of high nervous tension, unusual in her, did not like this. There was a reason for the delay. Simier had been summoned back from the Low Countries, where his master was being military, in order to undertake this delicate mission; and he had paused at his ancestral mansion on the way only to find that his wife was having an affair with his younger brother. He did not kill the brother with his own hands, for that would have been sinful, but caused him to be cudgeled to death by servants. Soon after that the erring wife died—suddenly.

When Jean de Simier finally arrived in England and made his bow before Elizabeth, who did not know about this business, he bore with him two thousand crowns' worth of jewels for bribery and also a letter from Alençon addressed to Elizabeth as "Perfect Goddess." Alençon asked only for a throne, £60,000 a year, freedom of worship, and one of the larger duchies, say York or Lancaster, together with all its properties, appurtenances, and income.

Elizabeth delighted in Simier. She tweaked his nose and dug a thumb into his ribs, while with an audacity that made the English gasp he poured love-words over her like syrup. Elizabeth had a fondness for nicknames: Dudley was her "eyes," Oxford her "boar," Christopher Hatton her "lids" or else her "sheep," or "mutton," or "bell wether," while Sir Walter Raleigh she sometimes called her "jumping jack," sometimes, possibly in reference to his flat Devonshire accent, her "water." Many court jokes and puns revolved around these nicknames. A note containing the picture of a bucket or ewer meant Raleigh. Hatton signed many of his letters with pen quirks meant to represent downcast eyes. And now this new man, Simier, whom she dubbed her *petit singe*, her "little monkey," decorated *his* many letters to Elizabeth with X's and with pairs of entwined arrow-pierced hearts.

Elizabeth, as she simpered and blushed, sidewise watching the situation in the Low Countries, must have known that almost nobody would believe her at first. She fooled them, acting with what was for her alacrity. She consulted physicians and was proclaimed to be capable of bearing a child. She consented to the appointment of commissioners to arrange the marriage terms.

Her councilors tried to talk her out of it, thus reversing the roles of the past. She snapped like a terrier.

The public did not fancy the marriage at all. They loved their Queen, and they would like to see her happy, but—well, a Spaniard had been bad enough, a Frenchman would be worse. And this wasn't even much of a Frenchman.

These murmurs she may never have heard, but she did see the pamphlet John Stubbs wrote, and it threw her into a rage. She had Stubbs arrested, along with Singleton, the printer, and Page, the seller of the pamphlet, which opposed the marriage. She strove to have them hanged, but this was impossible. She spluttered that her fiancé had been insulted. She got lawyers to drag out an old law (1 & 2 Philip and Mary, cap. ii) that had been passed specifically for the protection of her brother-in-law, in it called "the Queen's husband." She declared that Alençon was to all intents and purposes her husband, and that therefore the law applied in this case. She carried her point. Page was acquitted, but Singleton and Stubbs were sentenced to loss of the right hand. Except in times of national ferment, when tempers were at boiling point, there was little of this sort of medievalism any more. It scarcely seemed possible that the Queen would go through with it.

She did. Stubbs and Singleton were taken to a stand before the palace at Westminster, November 3, 1579. The crowd was large, but it was sullen, silent. The sentence was carried out with cleaver, beetle, and red-hot iron. Singleton, while they cauterized his stump, looked at what he had lost. "I have left there a true Englishman's hand," he said. Stubbs took off his hat with his left hand. "God save Queen Elizabeth," he cried, then fainted from loss of blood.

"She'll get over it," troubled courtiers muttered. "Wait till she *sees* the man."

He came. In disguise, strictly incognito, his presence not known to more than a few thousand, he was smuggled into the palace, where Elizabeth had rooms prepared for him; and he bowed to her.

She gushed; yet in nothing she did was she more effusive than her Frog. She had that name for him almost instantly—the Frog. She might sometimes refer to him as her Moor or her little Italian, because of his complexion, but mostly he was her Frog, warts and all. A bull frog, he had an unexpectedly deep voice. It must be admitted that he hopped well.

He was in the palace for only two days, and then he was smuggled out; on his way back to France he wrote no fewer than three rapturous letters to the light of his life. The French commissioners in London to arrange a first draft of her marriage treaty declared afterward that they had not even known of the Duke's presence. It is possible. He was in and out of the Queen's rooms a great deal, as she was in and out of his, at all hours. They billed and cooed. They were ridiculous.

"But I shall not be satisfied," wrote Simier to a friend, "till the curtain is drawn, the candles out, and Monsieur fairly in bed."

There were many others who felt the same way. Alençon, with the approval of Elizabeth, had lately accepted the sovereignty of the Low Countries, and she had promised to help him, mostly with money. But when the marriage commissioners finished their work and it was agreed that it must be ratified by the principals within two months or cease to be effective, she shilly-shallied shamelessly, permitting the two months to pass.

The great, tight-stretched, black fear of a Catholic league that would crush all else beside itself had not passed. But since the climax of the St. Bartholomew massacres and gradual realization that these had not meant the beginning of a long-planned vengeance, the fear had subsided somewhat. France at least would be more acceptable than Spain.

Spain glowered now, and with reason. Drake had returned from his trip around the world with such a treasure as had never before been seen, and the new Spanish Ambassador, the aging aristocrat, scholar, and ex-cavalry officer Don Bernardino de Mendoza, had been vehement in his demands for restitution. The treasure had been lodged in the Tower, and in all probability it would never leave the country. Nevertheless, this was more serious than the seized loan of a dozen years back. This was out-and-out loot. The Queen wavered. She countered. She accused Spain of helping the rebels in Ireland. She had been the first offended, she must be the first repaid. When she had taken from that treasure the cost of her Irish war, *then* perhaps she would see what might be done with the change, if any.

These were bold words. Spain was stronger than ever. Only the other day, at the death of the King of Portugal without heirs, Philip, himself a pretender, had sent in Alva, who in just fifty-eight days overran and reduced all the rest of the Iberian peninsula, a campaign that made men's heads reel.

Portugal, in addition to containing Lisbon, the best port on the Atlantic coast, claimed immeasurable territories in Asia, the East Indies, the Americas. All these, and all the wealth they represented, would now belong to that somber small man in the Escorial.

It was too much. Something had to be done. Elizabeth sighed and sent again for her Frog. *This* time, she vowed, she was in earnest.

He came, and the farce was renewed at a quicker tempo, a higher pitch. The court, never staid, now seethed. Alençon would thump his chest, such as it was, and swear to heaven that he adored the Queen; and he'd spray her hands and wrists with kisses, while she sighed. Once she wailed that to marry him would be to assume for England the responsibility of invading the Low Countries, something she was loath to do unless France proclaimed a willingness to share the burden. Promptly from Paris came word that Henri III, upon news of the marriage, would pledge all conceivable cooperation. Once Elizabeth cried in tragic tones that though her heart was broken, her council had forbidden the marriage because of the Frog's religion. Alençon promptly and publicly declared that he would change over. Once he whipped out a dagger and held it to his heart, crying that he would kill himself if she did not promise right here and now to wed him; but he did not carry out this threat, and soon he was in tears again. Whenever he wept, which was rather often, Elizabeth could handle him.

Betting in the city continued at three to one against the marriage, but those closest to Elizabeth were beginning to have their doubts, for they had never seen her like this.

The greatest danger—and this was a dangerous game she played—was that France might be pressed too hard. Catherine de' Medici was not overly sensitive in political matters, but even she could be pricked too forcefully. After all, Alençon was her son. If he were made the laughingstock of Europe, his mother might in a rage throw power to the Guise faction, which would mean an alliance with Spain and the invasion of Scotland.

The odds on the marriage did not rise when shortly after the Frog's second Channel crossing Campion, Sherwin, and Briant, priests who had been captured in dramatic circumstances, at last were hanged and quartered. The story current at the time, and repeated by certain Catholic writers, was that Elizabeth had them hustled to the gallows in order to disconcert her suitor and show him how independent she was. This is a shameful slander. Elizabeth had known Edmund Campion personally, and now she pleaded with him to announce recognition of her authority in matters ecclesiastical as well as secular. He of course refused. The sentence that followed was unavoidable. The executions, far from being put forward, were postponed for a week in order to permit an appeal to Alençon to intervene—an appeal that was refused.

Encoiled in a many-tentacled argument, and cheerfully sure of herself at first, Elizabeth was insisting that France concede this, grant that. The promptitude with which her demands were met made her suspicious. She might well have been worried inwardly, for it began to look as if the Frog was here to stay; but she kept her composure. She was not fazed even when the French Ambassador, Castelnau, bluntly told her that everybody believed she was having an affair with Alençon. All the more reason to marry him, she said.

It was this same Michel de Castelnau, Sieur de Mauvissière, who waited upon the Queen the morning of November 22, 1581, at Greenwich. He confronted her in the gallery, backed by attendants, her arm linked in that of her suitor. He told her that his master, King Henri, through him wished to ask Her Majesty right out: Was she or was she not going to marry Monsieur?

"You may give your master this answer," said Elizabeth, and put her arms around Alençon and kissed him on the mouth. Then she drew a ring off one of her fingers and put it on one of his. Turning, she introduced him to the ladies and gentlemen as their future master.

At last something definite seemed to have been done. Henri III acted swiftly, dispatching a commission to arrange final details. The commission found the Queen undecided. An hour after the scene on the gallery she'd had Dudley into her closet and told him that by hook or crook he must get that ring back. The Frog had surrendered it, though he was furious.

Now she admitted that all her terms had been met, but she asked what security she had that those terms would be carried out. She ought to have some substantial security—Calais, say.

Catherine de' Medici must have swallowed hard. They had expected Elizabeth to be trying: they had not expected anything as bad as this. But it was agreed to. All right, then, Calais.

This could be a tremendous triumph for Elizabeth, who had been striving for many years, and in many ways, to get Calais back. But now if she took it, she'd have to take Alençon too. She raised her price. Calais *and* another city—Le Havre!

This was preposterous, as it was meant to be, and the negotiations ceased. But the Frog remained. After all, where was he to go? They didn't want him at home. He was overlord of the Low Countries, but he needed an army to get them. So he lingered, ignoring hints.

It was February before they got rid of him. Elizabeth gave him at least £25,000 cash. She begged him to be careful in the war. She was forty-eight then.

They corresponded constantly, and in the most extravagant terms. For two and a half years little Hercules did everything wrong, being more hindrance than help to the Huguenot cause, a mere annoyance to William of Orange. He died obscurely, of natural causes, in an unimportant castle.

Elizabeth wrote his mother a note of condolence. But her own, Elizabeth's, grief was the greater, she said, for whereas Catherine de' Medici had or had had other sons, Elizabeth had only the one husband.

She always referred to him as her husband.

She wore mourning for months.

XXIV

HER first twenty-five years had been spent in holding her breath, the next in the avoidance of war. At fifty, though men still babbled of her perfections, professing that they dared not look long upon her face any more than at the sun, she was no beauty. She wore a wig—a succession of wigs rather, most of them yellowish, slightly red. Such teeth as she had left were black, and her lips, always thin, and pale, failed to hide them. There was a touch of the claw now about hands that had once been so lovely. Toward the end of her reign she favored gloves, a rare refinement in those days. She probably had more gloves than anybody else in the world.

Nobody had expected her to last long; yet here she was, a grizzly kitten, still laughing, scolding, cracking jokes, lapsing now and then into those fits of vulgarity that so embarrassed her attendants, astounding foreigners, outshining everybody else in a court easily the most brilliant in Europe—here she was, now a goddess, again a guttersnipe, sharp, sarcastic, incredibly but most emphatically alive.

Where was the court? Ask rather: where was the Queen? What with pageantry, Latin speeches, the sending-ahead of harbingers, the acceptance of scrolls and gifts, the acknowledgment of bombastic welcomings, she did not move fast; but move she did, and with a restlessness that appeared to increase with age; while the court perforce moved with her. The fat ones might pant, but their mistress thrived on it. She was sixty-seven when, about to start on another summerful of progresses, she learned that there was grumbling at the prospect. This amused her mightily. Yet she was gracious. Let the old and feeble stay in the city if they wished, she said. The young ones could come along with her and keep her company.

England had no Versailles, no Escorial or Kremlin. Buckingham did not exist then, nor did Sandringham, and the Windsor of the days before George IV was a modest pile. There were noblemen as sumptuously lodged and multitudinously attended as the Queen herself. The royal palaces—and there were many—were comfortable country houses, not notably pretentious. Much more than at the present, London dominated England. Twenty times larger than the town next in size, and still growing fast, it was a cesspool, a place of plagues, abominably overcrowded. The Queen displayed not only her fondness for hawking and hunting but also common sense when she preferred the country homes. She had been born at Greenwich; she was to die at Richmond. She did not like Hampton Court, once a favorite, after her near-death of smallpox there. It has been remarked that she seldom revisited Hatfield, her first household, and the suggestion is that this was because it held unhappy memories for her. Perhaps. It could also be pointed out, however, that Hatfield was a small seat, hardly capable of accommodating the English court. Nor was it on Thames, an important point.

Wherever she was, the whole great process of government revolved around her. If there was in those days nothing like the elaborate ceremonial and the trappings that encrust the English court today, this could have been in part because Elizabeth was simply too busy.

Yet she could shine! The German traveler Hentzner saw her at Greenwich:

"We were admitted by an order, which Mr. Rogers had procured from the Lord Chamberlain, into the presence-chamber hung with rich tapestry, and the floor, after the English fashion, strewed with hay [rushes], through which the Queen commonly passes in her way to chapel. At the door stood a gentleman dressed in velvet, with a gold chain, whose office was to introduce to the Queen any person of distinction that came to wait on her. It was Sunday, when there is usually the greatest attendance of nobility. In the same hall were the Archbishop of Canterbury, the Bishop of London, a great number of counsellors of state, officers of the crown, and gentlemen, who waited the Queen's coming out, which she did from her own apartment when it was time to go to prayers, attended in the following manner: —

"First went gentlemen, barons, earls, knights of the Garter, all richly dressed and bareheaded; next came the Lord High Chancellor of England, bearing the seals in a red silk purse, between two, one of whom carried the royal sceptre, the other the sword of state, in a red scabbard, studded with golden fleur-de-lis, the point upwards; next came the Queen, in the 65th year of her age (as we were told), very majestic; her face oblong, fair but wrinkled; her eyes small, yet black and pleasant; her nose a little hooked, her lips narrow, and her teeth black (a defect the English seem subject to, from their too great use of sugar); she had in her ears two pearls with very rich drops; her hair was of an auburn colour, but false; upon her head she had a small crown, reported to be made of some of the gold of the celebrated Luneburg table; her bosom was uncovered, as all the English ladies have it till they marry; and she had on a necklace of exceedingly fine jewels; her hands were slender, her fingers rather long, and her stature neither tall nor low; her air was stately, her manner of speaking mild and obliging. That day she was dressed in white silk, bordered with pearls the size of beans, and over it a mantle of black silk shot with silver threads; her train was very long, the end of it borne by a marchioness; instead of a chain, she had an oblong collar of gold and jewels. As she went along in all this state and magnificence, she spoke very graciously, first to one, then to another (whether foreign ministers, or those who attend for different reasons), in English, French and Italian: for besides being well skilled in Greek, Latin and the languages I have mentioned, she is mistress of Spanish, Scotch and Dutch. Whoever speaks to her, it is kneeling; now and then she raises some with her hand. While we were there, William Slawata, a Bohemian baron, had letters to present to her; and she, after pulling off her glove, gave him her right hand to kiss, sparkling with rings and jewels—a mark of particular favour. Wherever she turned her face as she was going along, everybody fell down on their knees. The ladies of the court followed next to her, very handsome and well-shaped, and for the most part dressed in white. She was guarded on each side by the gentlemen pensioners, fifty in number, with gilt halberds. In the ante-chapel, next the hall where we were, petitions were presented to her, and she received them most graciously, which occasioned the acclamation of *God save the Quene Elizabeth:* She answered it with *I thancke you myn good peupel.* In the chapel was excellent music; as soon as it and the service were over, which scarcely exceeded half-an-hour, the Queen returned in the same state and order, and prepared to go to dinner."

The nation was getting rich. England made no conquests, planned none. The land was subject to famines, caused usually by drought, such as in the middle 1590's; and the fisheries had declined; but new industries were being developed—especially the textile industry, encouraged by swarms of Protestant refugees from the Netherlands who brought with them not only their skills but often their machinery as well. There was poverty, there were slums, and the countryside still was infested with outlaws; but the people on the whole were prosperous and growing more so. Elizabethan England is thought of for its dash and color, and of course for its drama. It also had its counting-houses. Take Cecil. Posterity has put him down as a plotter, a power behind the throne, one who moved the marionettes in the international game of diplomacy. But it should be remembered that at least three quarters of Cecil's work—and he was a prodigious worker—had to do with the betterment of commercial relations between England on the one side, Scandinavia, the Low Countries, Spain, France, and the lands of the Mediterranean on the other.

As yet English mercantilism headed east, the seas off the Americas being no more than a pirate's playground. They were alert, those old-time merchants. When Copenhagen boosted tariffs, English ships bypassed it for German ports on the Baltic. A trade with Muscovy was developed, then one with the Orient, largely by land, by caravan. When the Pope forbade dealings with the infidel Turk, the Italian cities suffered, but there were

English and Huguenot vessels to make the run, and Cornwall found a new market for its tin.

Elizabeth has been upbraided for her parsimony. Historians assert that by a judicious expenditure here and there she would have saved a great deal more in the long run, and that her escape from such-and-such, in view of the heart-chilling stinginess with which she prepared for it, or failed to prepare, was sheer luck. It may be. The fact remains that the land she found poor she left prosperous. The world knew this. Philip of Spain, potentially the world's wealthiest monarch, was paying eighteen per cent on loans from the Fuggers, the Spinolas, the Malvendas, Dorias, De Looes, Pallavicines, LaFranchis, from virtually every large banking-house in Europe. Elizabeth got all she wanted at eight or nine per cent.

In everything else it was as though the harder she ran, the more she stayed in one place. The church from which all her pretensions were pendant had not advanced either in its revenues or in the hearts of its communicants, and truly it was in a parlous state, being threatened by a reinvigorated Catholicism now at last equipped with that sharpest of all weapons, the martyr. Foreign affairs appeared to be about where they had been twenty-five years earlier, with this difference: nations that previously had been inclined to view Elizabeth with mixed amusement and scorn, not taking her too seriously, now looked at her with distrust and with fear. (Though broken promises bobbed like eggshells in the wake of her career, she was always dismayed when foreigners did not believe her.) The long-dreaded Catholic invasion was closer than ever. The Duke of Guise was raising forces for the purpose in France, Bavaria, and the Low Countries, the plan this time being to strike England directly rather than by way of Scotland. This venture of course had the blessing of the Vatican. The only thing holding it up was Philip, who was trying to decide whether to take over the whole task himself.

"The realm is ripe for revolution," Mendoza wrote to his master in 1583. "It is full of sects and factions. . . . There is every reason therefore to expect success" in the great undertaking.

Mendoza, though more cunning and also more careful than any of his predecessors, inevitably was the centerpiece of all Catholic plottings in England, and as inevitably was found out. He in his turn was summoned before an icy-eyed council and told to leave. They were more accommodating with him than they had been with de Spies: they gave him fifteen days. He was succeeded by a man who did not have plenipotentiary powers or the rank of ambassador but was a mere commercial factor, Don Antonio de Guaras; but soon he too got mired in treason and, after spending a term in the Tower, was deported. Meanwhile the English Ambassador at Madrid had also been handed his passport. Thereafter, though there was still no declaration, it was understood by all that the two nations were at war.

A specter that had been haunting English statesmen for a long while was more than ever in evidence now—the specter of assassination. Almost anybody could get to Elizabeth at almost any time. She scorned to take precautions, though the men who had sworn to kill her must have been numbered in the scores, some of them crackpots, but others professional bravoes. "Illegal murder" was in the air anyway: of late there had been

Darnley, Lennox, Guise, Coligny, Rizzio, Murray, and many others, and soon the current Duke of Guise would be so erased, and immediately afterward, by way of revenge, Henri III. What more tempting target than Elizabeth? Philip and His Holiness were offering rewards—dispensations, estates, lump sums, orders, titles. True, the assassins were a clumsy lot who missed more often than they hit, for they seemed obsessed with the notion that they must use a new, tricky, unreliable mechanism, the pistol, rather than a knife, as their grandfathers or an Italian would have done. But they kept coming. It was the *fifth* bribed pistoleer who on a July night in 1584 at last successfully got to William of Orange.

England stood stunned. Elizabeth had done precious little to help William the Silent, the heart and soul of the revolt in the Netherlands. Alençon had died only a month before. The danger now was that the discouraged Dutch, pressed hard by Parma, would give up.

William of Orange, like the Earl of Murray, like Admiral Coligny, all of them shot, had made up England's first line of defense. So long as they were still fighting, Elizabeth didn't need to do so.

The men of England, or a great many thousands of them, virtually all those of high rank, signed an extraordinary document, the Bond of Association. It was a statement of their determination to keep off the English throne any person whose claim thereto might have been brought about directly or indirectly by the violent death of Queen Elizabeth. The thing was probably illegal. Nothing like it had ever before been framed. A good many must have signed because they were afraid to refuse; but still it stood as a warning, and it was more or less regularized when Parliament passed a somewhat similar if weaker resolution in the form of a law, 27 Eliz., cap. i. This could not be called a tribute to Elizabeth herself. It was an organized recognition of the peril in which the realm stood. Elizabeth would never have any children now. When she died, every holder of public office would be without authority, every military man too. All contracts would be nullified or at least held in a state of suspension. Nothing could move. Mary might succeed her, and Mary was a Catholic, a vindictive one. Mary's only child was King James of Scotland, who, though he had flirted with the Pope, yet remained technically a Protestant. Almost anything might happen, accompanied by violence.

The piecing together of a torn-up letter, some brilliant spy work, some patient deciphering, and a good deal of torture—and the government became aware of the latest plot, the one to bring Guise over, in all its details. It was elaborate, but in essential features the same as the others. It included the assassination of Elizabeth and the proclaiming of Mary, who never denied that she knew about it. Had Philip not been so slow to make up his mind, the thing might have been done before the councilors had any hint of it. Now all sorts of precautions were taken, and there was a great deal of hanging.

Mary still was permitted to live. Elizabeth, almost the only non-Catholic in the realm who was opposed to the finishing off of this troublesome guest, may have thought that Mary alive, as a hostage, helped to *prevent* such an occurrence. This is not likely. Still less likely is it that Elizabeth was stirred by a feeling of friendliness. By this time the two women, who never met, had come to hate each other. It is most probable that Elizabeth still staunchly thought of Mary as a semi-sacred person, an anointed queen who must not be judged by commoners.

A few years back Mary's household allowance, paid to her by the English government, had been cut from £52 to £30 a month. It seems to have been a routine move to trim expenses, and caustic remarks have come only from those who forget that the lady had £12,000 a year in her own right, paid regularly from France, the greater part of which went into machinations aimed at Elizabeth. Mary was moved to meaner quarters, for safety's sake. Shrewsbury's successors, Sir Ralph Sadler and later Sir Amyas Paulet, were stern puritans, and Tutbury was a drear place where she was denied an outside room for fear she'd climb out the window or at least use it for signaling to friends. Notwithstanding, her spirits were high. She still believed, and with much reason, that she would soon be Queen of England.

Then another plot was exposed, and Mary was in this one too, right up to the ears. The statesmen moved. Even Elizabeth moved.

XXV

MARY STUART never forgave her enemies or failed her friends, being in this the opposite of her "dear sister" Elizabeth, who was at all times willing to let bygones be bygones, though she was ready too, whenever policy or her own *amour propre* suggested, to deliberately disown a faithful follower. At Shrewsbury's home, where most of her exile was spent, Mary kept considerable state. Though there can be no question of the loyalty of her host-and-keeper, neither can there be any doubt that Mary might have escaped almost any time she chose. But—where would she go?

There were times, moments of national emergency, or supposed emergency, such as the Spanish fleet scare in 1570 or the St. Bartholomew massacres, when the guard around Sheffield Castle was increased; but these spells never lasted long. There were other times when Elizabeth may have wished that her cousin *would* escape. There was at least one occasion when Elizabeth was in communication with the current regent of Scotland, the Earl of Mar, about a plan to hand Mary over. This fell through because Elizabeth, who was getting worried about what posterity might think, insisted that Mar must first give her a written guarantee that Mary would not be hurt (she knew perfectly well they'd kill the woman: this was sheerly for show) and Mar refused.

No pressure had been brought to bear on Mary to change her religion, which was just as well, for while she was not much interested in church affairs, and surely no bigot, she would no more have deserted Catholicism than she would a servant in trouble. "I am not one of those that would change my religion every year," she said. It distressed her, largely no doubt for political reasons, that her child was being brought up a Protestant. She corresponded with him as soon as he could read. She agreed to share her shadowy authority with him so that he could truly be called King, though she reserved the right to withdraw this honor whenever she might see fit. At one time, when James was in his teens, their letters waxed affectionate. She sent him a sword, and when, delighted, he buckled it on, he spoke about someday winning his mother's crown back for her. A not attractive lad, he was pathologically conceited. His manners weren't good. As he cooled toward his mother, he warmed toward Elizabeth, with whom likewise he was in correspondence. He even concluded a treaty with Elizabeth (he was of age now) whereby she gave him a pension and half promised him the succession. Mary was not even mentioned in this treaty. She flew into a rage and disinherited James, solemnly naming as her successor to the English throne (but keeping this part of it secret, lest her income from France be cut off) Philip II of Spain, who indeed had a good claim, for he was a direct descendant of John of Gaunt.

It was in January of 1585 that Mary was moved to Tutbury. In the middle of April her new guardian, Sir Ralph Sadler, was replaced by an even sterner puritan, Sir Amyas Paulet. The following month Walsingham, the Queen's principal secretary, ordered Paulet to open all Mary's mail, both incoming and outgoing. She had not been permitted to receive mail direct, but only through the French Ambassador, and in September of that year the Ambassador decided to hold all her letters: as they were being opened, they might incriminate her. Cutting her only contact with the outside world was a cruel blow, but there was a purpose in it.

She spent almost a year, a dreary time, at Tutbury, and she gave a cheer when in December they told her that she was to be moved to Chartley Manor, twelve miles away. Chartley was moated and it was tolerably strong, but the neighborhood was Catholic, and the castle itself would be harder than Tutbury to guard. Sir Amyas Paulet objected to the shift. It was then necessary to tell him of the trap. He was one of six persons who knew.

Sir Francis Walsingham is our villain here. He looked the part too, judging from the National Gallery portrait. Long, lugubrious, black-bearded, dressed in black too, his ruff immaculate, he suggests a Satan with no sense of humor. We know almost nothing about the man personally. Like Cecil, he was a hard worker who suffered from poor health. He was a puritan. He spent his small private fortune in serving Elizabeth, who didn't like him, and when he went into bankruptcy she refused to help him, so that after his death he was buried at night in order to save the expense of a public funeral.

Walsingham had taken over from Cecil what we would call the intelligence department. He was one of the great detectives. He had spies everywhere, even one in the College of Cardinals. It is an indication of his ability that from this time Elizabeth, who previously had been unwilling to grant a penny to it, was spending £2,000 a year on secret service.

There was a young man named Gilbert Gifford who had been educated at the English Jesuit seminary at

Reims and who for some reason we do not know—
whether for money or vengeance or sheer perversity—
elected to betray his people. A baby-faced youth, not at
all sinister in appearance, he came from a distinguished
Catholic family whose seat adjoined Chartley. He knew
every foot of the ground in those parts, as he knew the
tradesmen of the locality, among whom his name went
far.

It was Gifford who found the brewer.

Chartley Manor did not have its own brewery, and a
villager got this trade. One barrel a week went to Mary's
household, pitifully small now. It was made known to
the prisoner—just how we can only guess—that if she
took the spigot out of that barrel she would find something interesting. She did—and fished up a waterproof
packet of letters.

Mary was experienced in deceit, and for all her eager-
ness she was cautious at first. But the thing seemed unbeatable. Gilbert Gifford's bona fides could not be questioned. Message after message was sent and received.
There was of course a great accumulation of letters at
the French embassy, and Mary herself had much to say.

Those in the secret were Gifford himself, who disappeared once things were set up; Walsingham; Elizabeth;
Paulet; Thomas Phelippes, a small, lean, yellow-haired,
short-sighted, pock-marked handwriting expert in Walsingham's employ; and the brewer, who collected from
both parties, at the same time raising the price of his
beer: he was known among the government group,
sardonically, as "the honest man," but his name does not
survive.

Phelippes was ostensibly a secretary of Paulet. He
knew Mary by sight and would bow to her when she

was wheeled around the garden: she suffered now from rheumatism. Phelippes would make a copy of each message, whether coming or going, and send the original on via messengers who were trustworthy Catholics; a professional forger, he was clever with seals. Then he would decipher his copies and dispatch them to Walsingham by messengers who did not know what they were carrying.

This was the way in which they gave Mary Stuart enough rope; and soon she did what they had expected.

To cavil about the evidence is to miss the point. True, Mary did not have a fair trial by present-day standards, but neither did anybody else in the sixteenth century. The question is not of details, of niceties, but one so vast that it embraces every other: *had they the right to try Mary at all?*

She was a monarch. Was she above man-made law?

Another element enters. There is a legal maxim, *Longa patientia trahitur ad consensum*—which is to say, prolonged tolerance gives consent. Many an Englishman must have asked himself: If they were going to kill her, why didn't they do it years ago? Mary had been toying with treason so long that she had come to be regarded as a landmark, a national institution.

The Babington conspiracy was different from many in that it was a home product, not inspired, as far as we know, by anybody from foreign parts. It counted on foreign aid, of course: they all did. Parma was to land his Spaniards at the signal of Elizabeth's murder.

Anthony Babington as a boy had been a page for Mary at Sheffield, and he adored her. He reserved for himself the honor of leading the party that would sweep down upon Chartley just as the slaughter at court was about to begin. For it was to be a carnage. All the principal ministers were to be wiped out. It must have given Walsingham a certain wry satisfaction, as he read the decipherments sent by Phelippes, to note that he himself was third on the list: Cecil was second, Elizabeth of course first.

About a dozen were directly involved, all young, all harebrained. Six were in more or less daily contact with the Queen. Elizabeth had been urged to weed out the court Catholics, or at least to make them take some sort of loyalty test. This she would not do. She could not believe that anybody who knew her would want to kill her.

There was no call to bring in Mary. Nothing needed to be done inside Chartley. When Babington wrote, via the beer barrel, to tell her the plan and ask for her approbation, it was undoubtedly for the purpose of winning a priceless treasure, her answer. Why she *did* answer, it would be hard to say; but she did. She was convicted largely on a copy of that letter, Phelippes's copy. It would not be admitted as evidence in a court today. It was perfectly proper then.

Weeks were to pass before all the names of the court youths could be learned. It must have been a temptation to spring the trap prematurely. These were wild lads, and if they learned that they were suspect, they might lug out and lay about them. It was hard enough on Walsingham, though he was naturally a lurker, a man well closeted. For Elizabeth, who was right out in the razzle-dazzle of the court, obliged to keep smiling, it must have been hell.

At the first arrest the culprits scampered every which way, but they were readily rounded up, convicted, and hanged. That was routine. The big thing was Mary.

It was decided to have her tried by a special high commission of peers. Many possible sites were discussed. The Tower? Elizabeth objected. Though London was predominantly Protestant, a crowd was a crowd and could too easily become a mob. Herford Castle? Grafton? Woodstock? Faults were found with each. Northampton? Huntingdon? Coventry? At last they selected Fotheringay, a strong, roomy castle, a crown property, in Northamptonshire. There in the large audience chamber on October 14, 1586, commissioners to the number of forty-odd confronted Mary.

She denied their jurisdiction, but when she was told that if she refused to appear she would be tried anyway, she consented to appear, though not to plead. She had no real defense except a flat denial. She was not permitted a lawyer. No defendant in such a case ever was. Anyway, why should Mary need one? She had been expecting this and was prepared for it, and no lawyer in the land could have done half as good a job as she herself did.

She was forty-three, almost forty-four, pale, badly swollen with rheumatism, and her hair was false. She had always had a way with men. But these men heard her, and convicted her. The vote was unanimous.

The only sentence permitted, death, could not be executed until the Queen signed a warrant.

Outwardly calm, or calm for her, Elizabeth had plenty to think about. Among Mary's papers, seized, were many letters from politicians who were beginning to turn, as they believed, toward the rising sun. Elizabeth read all these letters, and then—as Mary would have done if given the chance—she burned them. She never did anything openly about them, for she could make allowances, remembering those years at Hatfield. Nevertheless she knew now.

More important, more immediate too, was the death warrant. It was her manifest duty to sign it. The whole privy council pleaded with her; the bishops pleaded with her. Parliament was summoned, a holdover body strongly puritanical; and it too—the Lords, of course, had already committed themselves at Fotheringay— voted unanimously to petition the Queen to sign the death warrant.

It was argued that Henri III of France would not dare to avenge his sister-in-law: any such move would play into the hands of the Guises and of Spain, that Catholic league of which Henri had almost as great a fear as had Elizabeth.

Scotland, men cried, could not move. All James sought was the English throne after Elizabeth was dead, and did not this make it certain for him? Granted, to ask James to subscribe to the execution would be *contra bonos mores*, but he knew what was being considered, and who had heard his voice? Mary herself had virtually no party left in Scotland.

There were those who whispered that some compromise would be reached—that Mary would be locked in a truly deep dungeon and allowed no visitors for the rest of her life. There were others who shook their heads and said that the only prison that could hold Mary Stuart was the grave.

Elizabeth fluttered like a caught bird. Desperate, she even listened to a suggestion that Mary be poisoned, and

Sir Amyas Paulet was sounded out about this. His reply was noble: "My good livings and life are at her Majesty's disposition and I am ready to so lose them this next morrow, if it shall so please her, acknowledging that I hold them as of her mere and most gracious favor, and do not desire to enjoy them but with her Highness' good liking. But God forbid that I should make so foul a shipwreck of my conscience, or leave so great a blot to my poor posterity to shed blood without law or warrant."

"The daintiness of these precise fellows!" Elizabeth is said to have exclaimed.

It was not until February 1 that she got around to signing the warrant, almost four months after Mary's conviction. Those responsible for its execution knew that she might change her mind again at any moment, and they hurried off to Fotheringay.

The decapitation took place in the great audience hall there in the presence of a large crowd of nobles and gentlemen, February 8, 1587.

As everybody had known she would do, Mary died beautifully.

Elizabeth wailed. She protested that she had never really meant to have that warrant served—a fiction that fooled nobody. Davison, the secretary who carried the warrant, was forced to pay a fine that ruined him, and spent a year in the Tower besides. Elizabeth raged. She could get no ordinary business done. For months she wouldn't even talk to Cecil. She ordered the court into mourning. She caused Mary's remains to be buried with royal honors at Peterborough Cathedral.

France wavered, the populace clamorous; but in time it subsided.

The Scots, who would gladly have killed Mary themselves, were furious to see another people do so. There would have been a war, had their King given the word.

James? His pension was raised, after which his complaint sank to a quiet croak, hardly heard. James had buckled on that mother-sent sword but once, to see if it fitted. It didn't.

XXVI

PHILIP has been likened to a spider; but he was not venomous, and his victims were victims only by blundering chance, not design, for he had no interest in them. Yet his *persistence* was spiderlike. The insect observed by Robert the Bruce was never more dogged than this lean and careful King of half the world.

England had signed a treaty with the Netherlands (August 10, 1585), most of the thirty-odd clauses of which seemed designed to keep someone from stealing something; but it was a recognition of the Low Countries as independent. This in itself was an insult to Spain. Nevertheless, Elizabeth insisted that she sought peace. In his plodding way Philip had begun to prepare for war, a real war, a big one. He was willing, however, as part of those preparations to talk about the possibilities of peace.

Again Elizabeth had declined to accept overlordship of the Low Countries, but she did agree to mediate in quarrels between towns or between towns and provinces, to appoint an admiral of the combined fleets, and to give military aid.

Her idea of the last was Dudley, who made an unholy mess of the job. The English still were not soldiers. They lacked experience, discipline. The Low Countries and, to a lesser extent, France had proved a good training ground for such groups as Elizabeth permitted to go. The best of them, "Black John" Norris, even without the similarity of nicknames, recalled the only other first-rate military man England had until this time sent across the Channel—Edward of Woodstock, the "Black Prince." Dudley antagonized and humiliated Norris, but then he did as much to almost everybody involved, so that Dutchmen grew choleric at the very thought of him, and even doting Elizabeth at last acceded to demands to recall him. But the damage had been done. Immense sums of money had been expended—dear Robin was nothing if not wasteful—and what had remained of Dutch confidence was gone entirely. The Spanish viceroy in the Low Countries, Parma, who, now that Alva was dead, could be called the first captain in Europe, picked up town after town. Beyond doubt he could have crushed the Dutch and swept the English into the sea, had it not been for direct orders from Philip that he spare his best troops, re-equip them, and keep them at hand for a Channel crossing.

For Philip had at last decided that instead of stamping out revolt in the Low Countries first and taking over England afterward, the task would be best done the other way around. He wasn't going to trust to Guise, who in any event would be busy in France, where still another civil war was making up. He would do the thing himself.

Philip was slow, not to say ponderous, but he was thorough. Parma set about segregating his best troops, getting them encamped near convenient ports, gathering barges. At the same time Santa Cruz, the Spanish Admiral, was building, assembling, rearming, and refitting ships and enlisting seamen in a dozen coastal cities of Portugal and Spain. The Armada was coming into being.

All this time Elizabeth prated of peace and let the Royal Navy go to pot. As for the fighting men so laboriously trained by Norris, by Peregrine Bertie, Sir Roger Williams, and others, these were shipped back in great batches, penniless, half starved, their pay more than a year in arrears, their clothing in rags, to be dismissed with, at most, a word of thanks.

What Philip lacked was money, and this he sought from the Pope, Sixtus V, who had the heaviest treasure chest in Europe. Sixtus thought it might be better to work a little longer on the young King of Scots, James. (It had long been a fond belief in upper Vatican circles that James, whom they knew only by mail, was teetering on the verge of conversion.) Philip answered testily that even if James did enter the One True Church, they could never be sure of the boy; but they *could*, he pointed out, be sure of *him*, Philip. Not that he wanted England for himself. He planned to give it to one of his daughters.

Sixtus, parsimonious, hedged. It was only after many months of the most degrading sort of haggling and wirepulling that he consented to put up one third of the cost, at the same time agreeing to give Philip a free hand with the English succession. A million crowns, then, as a first payment; but not one real, Sixtus added firmly, until an army had been put ashore in England.

All this Elizabeth, if she knew it, ignored. Still set on peace, she appointed commissioners, one of them Cecil's undersized second son Robert, and there were many conferences on the continent; but nothing came of them. Still she persisted. Cecil himself, who had written: "A realm gaineth more by one year's peace than by ten years' war," drew up a side-by-side "table of considerations," listing arguments for and against a war. He found many objections—the risk that English Catholics might fail to support it, the cost, the unpopularity of aggressive action, the fact that the Spaniards were now good customers for English cloth, the uncertainty that Parliament would vote supplies—but his conclusion was that it would be best to fight, and fight now.

Elizabeth could not be convinced. While Philip slowly gathered his strength, she went on trying to get her treaty. The preparation of the Armada—more than a mere fleet, it was a great national movement, a crusade —could not be kept secret. "All that cometh out of Spain must concur in one to lie or else we shall be stirred very shortly with heave and ho," wrote a grim Howard of Effingham, Lord High Admiral. But Elizabeth forbade war preparations: they might frighten off Philip, who still dangled before her that treaty possibility, that carrot.

Howard should be more than mentioned. It could seem odd that Sir Francis Drake, so emphatically the first sailor of his time, was not Lord High Admiral. It would have been unthinkable then. It had been daringly democratic even to make Drake vice-admiral. The Lord High Admiral had to be a nobleman. Hence Howard. But this man was not a nincompoop, a gilded fop, diamonds in his ears but nothing between them. He had spent a lot of time at sea. He got things done. If he wasn't the sailor Drake was, he was sensible enough to see this and courageous enough to admit it and to act upon it. Howard's was the ultimate responsibility, but he let Drake have his head, backing him in everything.

The Navy then was a secondary, looked-down-upon service, an occasional branch of the Army. Sailors were not military men, but artisans, civilian employees. Honor still was everything, at least theoretically, and the idea that honor could be gained aboard a ship, a noisome, uncomfortable edifice, simply hadn't occurred to anybody. You had to be on a horse to win honor.

Sea battles there had been, yes; there were even written works on naval tactics; but these were Mediterranean matters, calling for calm water, for "long ships" rather than "round" ones. Galleys could be maneuvered like cavalry if the sea was right and they were not too far from shore, but they would of course be useless in the open ocean. And except for galleys, a ship was thought of as a means to move soldiers. If there *had* to be a fight on the water, the thing to do was bring one's ship alongside an enemy ship so that the soldiers could engage. A ship, that is, was not thought of as a weapon but as a floating battlefield, or part of such a battlefield.

These considerations are important in any narrative of the Spanish Armada, history's first demonstration of a sea fight in the present sense of the phrase.

Few understood this at the time, and Elizabeth could not be expected to understand it. That she was persuaded to let Drake take a fleet down to the Spanish coast and knock out some of the shipping is saying a lot for her. It was a bold project, well in advance of current military thinking. Note again that Howard supported his second-in-command in this venture, though he himself was obliged to stay at home. If it succeeded, Drake would get the glory; if it failed, Howard would get the blame. That the best defense lies in taking the offensive was a conception of war beyond Elizabeth. When she came to her senses, she must have thought she'd been mad, or badly gulled, for she sent a messenger galloping to Plymouth with an order to call the whole business off. Drake, however, knew his Queen, and he had slipped away. At

ELIZABETH I 175

the mouth of the Channel he met dirty weather that might ordinarily have turned him back, but now he held on.

It is known as the Cadiz Raid. It was much more than that. Drake had thirty vessels, only six of them being Royal Navy ships. The largest, his flagship, the *Bonaventura*, six hundred tons, was smaller than the smallest of the sixty-five warships Spain either had built or was building for the Armada. The rest were armed merchant vessels, privately financed. Drake went into the harbor at Cadiz, sank a galleon, fought off a fleet of galleys, and, staying just outside the range of the shore batteries, had the whole assembled merchant fleet at his mercy. He transferred to his own vessels an immense quantity of stores intended for the Armada at Lisbon, mostly wine, corn, biscuits, dried fruits. He burned the rest. On April 21, 1587, he sailed out of Cadiz without having lost a man.

Having heard that a fleet from the Mediterranean was coming to reinforce the Armada, he made for Cape Saint Vincent to intercept it. Needing water, he set men ashore at Faro and stormed and took the fort. He picked up a convoy of store vessels headed for Lisbon, loaded with galley oars and cask staves, and these he burned. When the Mediterranean fleet failed to appear, he dismantled the fort at Faro and set sail straight for Lisbon itself. That the Spaniards were gathered there in overwhelming force he knew; yet he proposed to go in and blast them. The more there were, he pointed out to a council of war, the nearer together they'd be and therefore the easier it would be for fire to spread from one to another. The plan was a breathtaker, even for men who had previously served under Francis Drake, but it might have succeeded—had not dispatches now reached him from London. These were not so bad as the orders he'd slipped away from at Plymouth, but they forbade him to attack the Armada at its heart, Lisbon.

He lay under Cintra, picking up prizes. He sent in a flag to Santa Cruz (his orders did not specifically forbid this, something Elizabeth had probably never dreamed of) and challenged him to come out and fight. On the open sea, spread, the Spanish Admiral's vast advantage in numbers would be more telling; even so, Santa Cruz, though it must have pained him to do so, said no. His vessels were not properly stocked, his men not properly trained. So Drake sailed for Corunna, a place not mentioned in the orders. He swept the harbor of everything afloat, and sailed away again, laughing at the shore batteries, the galleys. In two months' time he had destroyed or caused to be destroyed about half the supplies Philip's men had spent the past three years collecting. But the hands had still to be paid. So he made for the Canaries and conveniently picked up a treasure carrack, the *San Pedro*. This was more than enough to pay for the whole expedition and give everybody a comfortable bonus besides, so he went home.

Here was a new way of waging war. Had Drake been permitted to practice it earlier (he had been clamoring to) and renew it afterward, Philip might have been kept off balance for years at such cost to himself that bankruptcy would at last have closed the matter without England's shores ever being threatened.

There had been various scares. Late in August of 1586 the report of a French landing in Sussex caused a near-panic, and only a week later the Governor of

Portsmouth reported having heard of ten thousand Spanish soldiers about to sail from Brittany.

As far as the Dutch were concerned, their greatest immediate alarm was that Elizabeth would sell them out. They had good reason for this fear. Spain assuredly would not grant a peace that didn't include a provision that England withdraw from the Low Countries, where, thereafter, all Protestantism would be stamped out and everything that the Dutch and Flemings had been struggling for these many long, bitter, black years would be thrown away. On the other hand, and largely because of the troubles, English-Dutch commercial relations had recently declined, whereas English-Spanish relations had never before been so brisk. Would the flag follow trade? It looked that way. As late as *a few weeks* before the Armada actually sailed, there were Dutch commissioners in London pleading with Elizabeth not to throw their country over by making peace with Spain.

Twice the Armada had been about to put forth. The original plan, worked out by a committee headed by Santa Cruz himself, had called for invasion in the summer of '87. Drake's doings had set this back—a whole year, Drake himself calculated. But extraordinary efforts were made, both in Iberia and in the Low Countries. By January, Parma had his thirty thousand men, his barges and supplies ready, and Philip ordered Santa Cruz to go ahead. A spell of unprecedentedly bad weather foiled this. The following month, Parma being still prepared, Philip gave the order again. And then Santa Cruz died.

On either of those occasions there would have been virtually no opposition at sea, and it was only at sea that

Spain feared anything. After Drake's success of the previous summer the Queen had let her seamen go, in order to save wages and food, and had dismantled all but two of the Royal Navy vessels, small ones in poor condition. There cannot be the slightest doubt that, had Santa Cruz not died when he did, England would have been invaded. Whether England would have been conquered, or rather whether it could have been *kept* conquered, is another question; but surely there would have been a bitter, bloody war.

Philip by and large was extremely well served. It was a time of magnificence for Spain—her golden age, when an amazing number of brilliant and memorable men in all walks of life caused her to gleam with an unforgettable light. All of these men were devoted to their monarch, and most of them were marvelously able. There had to be exceptions. When the Armada at last was ready to go and the admiral who had supervised its construction, who had masterminded the plan on which it was to be used, suddenly was snatched away—then it might be supposed that the second-in-command would be moved up. No such thing. The commander of so vast and holy an undertaking must be a man of high degree. The highest who was then available—it's true he knew nothing of naval matters—was the Duke of Medina Sidonia, who objected that he could not possibly handle such a job and begged to be excused. He was ordered to take command. He needed several months to get acquainted with the preparations and with his officers. It was May 19, 1588, before the greatest naval effort ever put forward by man at last sailed out of the Tagus.

It was made up of 150 vessels, 65 of them large warships, while 4 were huge galleases, 4 oversized galleys, 56 armed merchant vessels, and 20-odd caravels and pinnaces. (England in a frenzied last-minute spurt had mustered 38 naval vessels, only 13 being over four hundred tons.) There were 19,000 soldiers, some 1,000 gentlemen, about 2,000 priests and servants and such, besides the sailors and galley slaves, all of them confessed and shriven in advance, all forbidden to swear or to gamble; and there were no prostitutes.

Scattered by a blow, they reassembled at Ferrol, and on July 12, the weather now being mild, set forth again. Two weeks later they came in sight of the English, who had sailed out of Plymouth to meet them. The great moment had arrived. Philip got down on his knees. Elizabeth got up on her horse.

XXVII

FROM the first day of this lady's reign the question had entered every discussion of high politics: How many English Catholics would rise against the Crown if called upon? There were puritans who affirmed that the rebels would total less than ten per cent of the country's population. There were exiles, men like Dr. Allen, just created Archbishop of Canterbury to take office when Philip had conquered the land, who confidently and even clamorously asserted that at least ninety-five per cent of the people would spring to arms against the heretic queen the instant the Holy Father said the word. Sober statesmen tried to find a figure between these two that seemed sound. The condition of the roads, the scattering of Catholicism throughout thinly populated areas, the lack of reliable leaders, the absence of legal printed matter, fanaticism, just plain stupidity, spies—these combined with the fact that the Catholics themselves couldn't get along together (there were all sorts of factions, a city party, a country party, a French party, a Spanish one, Jesuits, anti-Jesuits, and others) to behaze the matter, blurring its outlines. The nearest thing to a test was the Rising in the North, but this had been a local affair, hobbled by family rivalries, taking place under feudal conditions, and because the Regnans in Excelcis bull had not yet been published, it had been executed by men with confused minds and split loyalties.

Thousands were promised. The Armada itself, besides vast supplies of food brought on the assumption that the retreating peasantry would adopt a scorched-earth policy, carried countless casques, muskets, breastplates, swords, for distribution to the faithful who would flock in. It was not expected that the military value of these liberated ones would be great, for everybody knew that during thirty years of peace the average Englishman had forgotten how to fight, but their nuisance value might be mighty.

The government had the same thought, and much of the preliminary planning centered around the possibility that the men might refuse to march far from home. It was one thing to drill on the village green, quite another to shoulder a musket and turn your back on a town that could be taken over in your absence by hitherto secret malcontents.

Thus it will be seen that both sides counted on a Catholic uprising in time of trouble and they were at variance only in their estimates of its size.

How many Catholics did rise? None.

When the Armada was sighted, horsemen rode off in all directions, and that night signal fires burned along the coast. Men made ready amid great excitement, but there was no disorder. These were stout volunteers, full of patriotic emotion, who probably would have fought with courage; but it must have brought tears to the eyes of the few real campaigners among them to think of what Parma's veterans, once landed, could do to them. A first-class commander, a Norris or Willoughby, might have made something out of them, even in the little time left. The man the Queen appointed, however, could have been picked by Philip himself, for he was no other than Robert Dudley, who would look so handsome in a helmet.

There was a small reserve army in London, intended

largely as a bodyguard for the Queen. Most of the men were assembled at Tilbury, some twenty thousand within the first few days and others pouring in all the time. This was the lowest point at which it was possible to cross the Thames conveniently, and the idea was to be prepared to meet Parma on either bank, for it was assumed that the Spaniards would strike at London.

It was at Tilbury that Elizabeth reviewed the troops, and a fine sight she must have made, on a spirited steed, her chin high, her hair flying in the breeze. This in itself was remarkable in a day in which princes, whether because of Oriental notions of seclusion or from ordinary prudence, generally avoided public places. But Elizabeth went further. She talked to the troops. She told them that she had every confidence in them and in their brave, upstanding commander. What's more, she had confidence in herself. "I know that I have the body but of a weak and feeble woman, but I have the heart and stomach of a king," she declared—and how they cheered her! "What fear was, I never knew," she told Parliament later.

Meanwhile the Navy was doing the real job. And not only the Navy but also every pirate, smuggler, or boated hotblood who felt like getting into the fight. Reports were spotty. Certainly a great deal of gunpowder was being burned. Never had there been such a noise! When a vessel put into port, perhaps with a prize, the sailors would have little time for talking, as there still was work to do out there: what they wanted was food, food, food, and also shot and powder. Elizabeth, despite all entreaties and the advice of experts, had insisted upon stocking her vessels with no more than a month's rations. These had been all but gone by the time the Spaniards hove into sight, in some cases had even been extended to six and seven weeks, so that the men were fighting on empty stomachs. All the same, they were fighting well.

More than five times as much gunpowder was burned by the English alone as had ever before been burned in any naval engagement, which in itself shows what a change had come over sea fighting. And still they pleaded for more.

It was not properly a battle. It was rather a hit-and-run affair, with the English, by far the faster sailers, refusing to grapple, though they got close enough to keep pouring in ball. Spanish soldiers lined the rails, weeping in rage, screaming curses, calling the Englishmen cowards, daring them to close and fight. But why should they? David would have been a fool to get caught up in Goliath's bearlike hug. He kept his distance. He cut in and out. He swarmed over the stragglers. Too fast to be caught, and much too cunning, the English clung to the Armada's flanks like a swarm of angry bees. No rest did they permit, no breathing-spell. When the Armada anchored off Gravelines the second night, the English sent in fire ships, and the Spaniards panicked and cut their cables, losing two anchors each, in most cases all they carried. By dawn the English had slipped into the anchorage, so that the dons couldn't get their hooks back.

"We pluck their feathers by little and little," gloated the Lord High Admiral.

They tried to force the Spaniards into the shallow waters off the French coast, and all but succeeded. Escaping, the demoralized dons necessarily backed into the North Sea.

Then God took over. "He blew with His wind, and they were scattered" is not strictly accurate, for the Spanish ships kept close together, sometimes too close, there being several collisions; but indubitably even before Drake, before Howard, or Frobisher, or any of the tried and attested heroes of this action, the Creator did the most toward victory.

Never had anybody known such weather, not the oldest fisherman. The whole of this four-day running fight had been carried on in fog and rainstorms, the days gusty under lowering skies, visibility almost zero, while the nights were black as ink. Indeed the Spaniards themselves attributed their defeat largely to the weather—that is, to God—and it was this more than anything else which broke their spirit. They would have battled any mere men, however numerous, however strong; but if the Almighty Himself was against them, how could they prevail?

Now a stiff southwester blew up, and the Armada, far from any friendly port, could scarcely turn into the teeth of it. The dons were too badly demoralized, or perhaps too badly led, to heave to and ride it out. They went with it, making for the north; and the English bees buzzed right after them.

The fear was that they might put into the Firth of Forth, conceivably by prearrangement with James. The Scottish King had been bribed to stay neutral by the promise of an English duchy (which promise Elizabeth blandly broke as soon as the Armada was smashed), but he might go back on his word, the double-dealing wretch.

The Spanish fleet did not put into the Forth, and the English broke off contact. They hated to do this, for they felt that they were missing a chance to win "the famousest victory that ever was in the world," but they could scarcely stand, they were so hungry, and they hadn't a grain of gunpowder left. When they last saw the Armada, it consisted of about 120 vessels, most of them seemingly sound, though in truth many were in pitiful condition: it was the damage done to their rigging by English shot, making them hard to handle, that as much as any one thing was responsible for the decision to round the northern tip of the island rather than fight back through the English fleet and re-establish contact with the mainland. The English sent two pinnaces to watch and report whether the dons put in at Denmark.

The dons didn't. In diminishing numbers because of collision and wreck, they skirted the Orkneys. They went aground. They foundered. They came down through the Irish Sea, losing ships right and left, all the survivors being slaughtered by the wild Irish. Only 54 vessels got back to Spain.

The Pope refused to pay his promised one third of the cost, because, as he pointed out, no army had been landed in England.

Meanwhile, it having been made certain that the Armada would not return south and that Parma could not cross from the Netherlands without heavy support, the English began putting their sick ashore. Not one English vessel had been lost, but while few Englishmen were wounded, many, because of bad beer and the absence of solid food, were faint and dizzy, so that they fell easy prey to scurvy. They were carried ashore by the hundreds, though there was no provision for them, and housed in any places their officers could find, often enough at the personal expense of those officers. Now that it was all over and they'd been laid off—for Elizabeth thought that she didn't need a Navy any longer, despite the tearful pleas of those who begged to be permitted to finish the job in Spain—a great many of them went to sleep and never woke up. "It would grieve any man's heart to see men who had served so valiantly to die so miserably," Lord Howard wrote to Cecil. The Lord High Admiral and Drake, his second-in-command, just before the coming of the Armada had taken it upon themselves to buy some extra provisions, fresh food, when the regular rations were weeks overdue. Now they were scolded for this, for the Queen was in the habit of going over all these accounts in person, figure by figure, and in the end they were obliged to pay for that food out of their own pockets.

Yet it must not for an instant be supposed that Queen Elizabeth was ungrateful. Clearly the hero of the occasion was the commander-in-chief of the forces in the field, Robert Dudley, Earl of Leicester. As a reward for his services, Elizabeth proposed to make him Lieutenant General of England and Ireland—that is, she proposed to give him more power than any English monarch had ever officially delegated to any subject. The howl of indignation that rose at the announcement didn't disturb her. She was so popular just then that she could have risked anything.

Dear Robin himself saved the situation by dying. There was the customary whisper about poison; it seems, however, he'd caught a cold on his way to Kenilworth, and complications ensued (he was a portly old party by this time, after all). The Queen, who certainly loved him, felt badly about it, but it's to be doubted that anybody else did. An epitaph said to have been written by Sir Walter Raleigh, though it was not engraved on the headstone, was much quoted:

Here lies the noble Warrior that never blunted sword;
Here lies the noble Courtier that never kept his word;
Here lies his Excellency that govern'd all the State;
Here lies the Lord of Leicester that all the world did hate.

XXVIII

THAT miserable man had meant more to her than anybody else in the world, the man she would have married, the one who took her back to childhood days, and who had shared her sufferings in London Tower. But she bore up. There was so much to be done. Time was what she wanted—and time was running out.

Still the despair of her own councilors, she was the wonder now of the civilized world. Marvelous tales were told of her. Exalted noblemen in foreign parts pulled strings in order to get an embassy to England so that they could have a look at this phenomenon. The populace cheered her wherever she went.

She enjoyed this. Her court was gay, there was always music, and never before had been seen such glittering clothes.

The Catholic league triumphed in France, a bad omen, but Henri III had submitted only until such time as he could arrange for the murder of the Duke of Guise, and this changed the whole picture. The extreme Catholics retaliated by having Henri assassinated, thus ending the Valois line, something Catherine de' Medici did not live to see, for she had died a few months earlier. Then a different Henri—Navarre, the Bourbon, a man of spirit, truly a Frenchman, debonair, gallant—had his sword out again. Navarre and Elizabeth seemed to understand each other. Although she had his family jewels for security, she hated to lend him money, all he ever asked of her; but she did lend it, and he did wonders with it. When after four years of fighting he decided to become a Catholic, thus reuniting his realm and gaining its capital for himself—"Paris is worth a Mass"—it did not notably shock anybody or overtip the balance of power.

Melancholy Walsingham had died a few years before that, and Warwick, Dudley's brother, and then Hatton, her "bell wether," and the incorruptible if somewhat henpecked Shrewsbury. Then Drake.

The year Drake died, the Spaniards made a raid on the English coast, their first and only one. From the point of view of high strategy it was hardly important. The town of Penzance was burned, also the village of Mousehole. Then the Spaniards were gone, never to return. But it showed that Philip still had fight in him.

Indeed, the very next year the second Armada set forth, almost as pretentious an affair as the first, but once again God was good to England, and this fleet was scattered and damaged beyond repair by a gale off Finisterre the fourth day out.

Lord Hunsdon died. He was her nearest relative and one of her closest friends. Then Cecil, the old reliable, the first member of her council, Cecil with his eyes that were like dirty blue water swirled in a bucket, his spade of a beard, his lists, averages, percentages. A month after that, Philip II himself died. Even her enemies were leaving her.

There was plenty of snarl left in the old lioness, though she laughed often too. She was sixty-three when a Polish Ambassador not only addressed her impertinently, but did so in very bad Latin. She rose to answer him in that same tongue, correcting him. Her reply was scorching, so that when she was finished the man wished he had never been born. Then she laughed, looking around: "God's death, my lords! I have been forced this day to scour up my old Latin." They loved her for things like that.

And she loved them. She was as crotchety as ever, but she had some mellow moments now, as when she told Parliament: "This Kingdom hath had many wise, noble, and victorious princes, but in love, care, sincerity, and justice I will compare with any prince that you ever had or will have." And again, to that same body: "I assure you, that though after my death you may have many stepdames, yet shall you never have a more natural mother than I mean to be unto you all."

Of course she still flirted. It was a fixed habit. She could no more have stopped flirting than stopped spitting. Raleigh, the well hated, the greatly feared, had been countered at court by one brought forward for that purpose—Robert Devereux, second Earl of Essex, a man who had everything, a petulant, impetuous lad, a latter-day Alcibiades, who caught her eye promptly and held it for years. She was frantically frolicsome then, and more than a little ridiculous. But she didn't mind, never had minded, if people laughed at her. When Essex waxed impertinent, she boxed his ears. When he waxed traitorous, she had his head off. It is certain that she hated to do this; but there was not the shilly-shallying of the old days. He was thirty-three at the time, she sixty-seven.

Cecil had two sons, the first something of a rake and never bright. The second, an undersized fellow named Robert, was as smart as the fondest father could wish, and he it was whom Cecil had trained to be his successor. Robert Cecil was a small, misshapen man, capable, earnest. When his father, still worrying, went to his reward, Robert was prepared to take over. He did this quietly, making no splash. The Queen, though she didn't like him, trusted him.

It could be that Robert Cecil got too presumptuous sometimes. When she was seriously ill and refused to go to bed, he had the temerity to tell her that she must. She looked down at him. "The word 'must' is not to be used to princes." However, she did go to bed, and they gathered around her while she lay for hours on end, and for days, a shrunken thing, staring at the draperies, finger in mouth. One morning, brightening, she called for music. "I verily believe that she means to die as gayly as she has lived," wrote an awed French Ambassador. But soon the finger went back into the mouth, and a puzzled frown touched her face, and after a while the musicians tiptoed out unnoticed.

Once she sat up suddenly. "I'm *not* mad!" she cried. "Tell them I'm *not* mad! I'm *not!*" They had some difficulty quieting her.

Everything had been arranged with James of Scotland, but a statement from the Queen herself would make things even safer. They pressed her to name a successor. She did not appear to hear them. James Stuart? She didn't stir. Navarre? Arabella Stuart? Huntington? Beauchamp? No sign. Suffolk? Here she opened her eyes. "I'll have no rascal's son in my seat!" Then she subsided, and with a sigh they went over the list once more, saying each name slowly, bending low, watching her. They said afterward that she had raised one hand a trifle when the name of the Scottish King was mentioned the second time. That was enough. Soon she wouldn't be in any position to contradict them.

For a long time she would not eat, but at last she accepted a few spoonfuls of broth.

She called for the Archbishop of Canterbury, and he knelt by her bed and prayed and prayed, his eyes fixed on a hand that hung out from under the bedcovers. He stopped, thinking that she was asleep. He started to get to his feet. But the hand was lifted a little, and the old man went on praying. When at last he slipped away, there was nothing moving in the room.

The night wore on. They were afraid to touch her. She had not spoken or moved for a long time.

Under a bedroom window was Robert Carey, her cousin, a lad she'd liked. Near him was a horse, saddled and ready, and all along the North Road, which led to Edinburgh, other horses were posted. Carey and his sister, Lady Scrope, had arranged a signal—a blue ring James himself had sent them for this very purpose. Carey wanted to be an earl, and the first person to give James the news would by custom be rewarded. So he waited, booted and spurred, watching the window where a dim light showed.

At three o'clock in the morning—it was March 24, 1603—Lady Scrope appeared at the window. She threw something out. Carey caught it: it was the blue ring. He mounted and was off. The Queen was dead, long live the King!

SELECTED BIBLIOGRAPHY

STANDARD HISTORIES

BLACK, JOHN B.: *The Reign of Queen Elizabeth, 1558–1603.*
BURNET, GILBERT: *History of the Reformation in England.*
BURTON, JOHN HILL: *History of Scotland.*
CHENEY, E. P.: *History of England from the Defeat of the Spanish Armada to the Death of Elizabeth.*
CLARENDON, EDWARD HYDE, FIRST EARL OF: *History.*
FROUDE, JAMES ANTHONY: *History of England from the Fall of Wolsey to the Defeat of the Spanish Armada.*
GREEN, JOHN RICHARD: *A History of the English People.*
LANG, ANDREW: *The History of Scotland.*
LAUGHTON, JOHN KNOX (ed.): *State Papers Relating to the Defeat of the Spanish Armada.*
LINGARD, JOHN: *A History of England.*
MOTLEY, JOHN LOTHROP: *The Rise of the Dutch Republic.*
PRESCOTT, WILLIAM H.: *History of Philip II.*

Surely the most entertaining of these is Froude. He had his faults, but being obvious they are easily discounted. Bishop Burnet is generally thought of as the "official" Protestant historian, Lingard as the "official" Catholic one. The newcomer to this field could not do better than Black, whose work is in one volume and of recent publication (Oxford, 1936).

LIVES OF ELIZABETH

AIKEN, LUCY: *Memoirs of the Court of Queen Elizabeth.*
ANTHONY, KATHARINE: *Queen Elizabeth.*
BEESLY, EDWARD SPENCER: *Queen Elizabeth.*
BEKKER, ERNST: *Elizabeth and Leicester.*
BIRCH, THOMAS: *Memoirs of the Reign of Queen Elizabeth, from the Year 1581 till Her Death.*
CAMDEN, WILLIAM: *The History of the Most Renowned and Victorious Princess Elizabeth, late Queen of England.*
CHAMBERLIN, FREDERICK: *The Private Character of Queen Elizabeth.*
CREIGHTON, MANDELL: *Queen Elizabeth.*
DARK, SIDNEY: *Queen Elizabeth.*
HUME, M. A. S.: *Two English Queens and Philip.*
———: *The Courtships of Queen Elizabeth.*
JESSOPP, AUGUSTUS: "Elizabeth" *(Dictionary of National Biography).*
MAYNARD, THEODORE: *Queen Elizabeth.*
MUMBY, FRANK A.: *The Girlhood of Queen Elizabeth.*
NEALE, J. E.: *Queen Elizabeth I.*
STRACHEY, LYTTON: *Elizabeth and Essex.*
STRICKLAND, AGNES: *The Life of Queen Elizabeth.*
WALDMAN, MILTON: *Elizabeth and Leicester.*
———: *Elizabeth, Queen of England.*
WIESENER, LOUIS: *The Youth of Queen Elizabeth.*
WRIGHT, THOMAS: *Queen Elizabeth and Her Times.*

If there were such a thing as a "standard" life of Elizabeth, it perhaps would be Bishop Creighton's, which is both full and fair. Among more recent publications the Maynard and Waldman biographies are recommended.

OTHER LIVES

ADDLESHAW, PERCY: *Life of Sir Philip Sidney.*
CHIDSEY, DONALD BARR: *Sir Humphrey Gilbert.*
———: *Sir Walter Raleigh: That Damned Upstart.*
CORBETT, JULIAN S.: *Drake and the Tudor Navy.*
DAKERS, ANDREW: *The Tragic Queen: a Study of Mary Queen of Scots.*
DE SELINCOURT, HUGH: *Great Raleigh.*
EDWARDS, EDWARD: *The Life of Sir Walter Raleigh.*
FULLER, THOMAS: *History of the Worthies of England.*
GOSLING, WILLIAM GILBERT: *Life of Sir Humphrey Gilbert.*
GOSSE, PHILIP: *Hawkins.*
HENDERSON, T. F.: *Life of Mary Queen of Scots.*
HUME, M. A. S.: *Philip II.*
———: *Sir Walter Raleigh.*
———: *The Great Lord Burleigh.*
KURKBAUM-SIEBER, MARGARETE: *Mary Queen of Scots.*
LANG, ANDREW: *The Mystery of Mary Stuart.*
McFEE, WILLIAM: *The Life of Sir Martin Frobisher.*
MUMBY, FRANK ARTHUR: *Elizabeth and Mary Stuart.*
———: *The Fall of Mary Stuart.*
NICHOLAS, SIR HARRIS: *Memoirs of the Life and Times of Sir Christopher Hatton, K.G.*
OBER, F. A.: *Life of Sir Walter Raleigh.*
PRESCOTT, H. F. M.: *Mary Tudor.*
RAIT, ROBERT: *Mary Queen of Scots.*
READ, CONYERS: *Mr. Secretary Walsingham and the Policy of Queen Elizabeth.*
RODD, SIR RENNELL: *Sir Walter Raleigh.*
SEDGWICK, HENRY DWIGHT: *Henry of Navarre.*
SKELTON, SIR JOHN: *Mary Stuart.*
SLAFTER, REV. CARLOS: *Sir Humfrey Gylberte and His Enterprise of Colonization in America.*

SMITH, ALAN GORDON: *William Cecil: the Power Behind Elizabeth.*
SMITH, CHARLOTTE FELL: *John Dee, 1527–1608.*
SPEDDING, JAMES: *The Letters and Life of Francis Bacon.*
STEBBING, WILLIAM: *Sir Walter Raleigh.*
STRICKLAND, AGNES: *Life of Mary Queen of Scots.*
TAYLOR, I. A.: *Sir Walter Raleigh.*
TYTLER, PATRICK FRASER: *Life of Sir Walter Raleigh.*
WALDMAN, MILTON: *Sir Walter Raleigh.*

Certain of the books listed above are much more than biographies. Admiral Corbett's, for instance, is unsurpassed as a history of one of the very great revolutions in naval warfare—that from oars-in-the-Mediterranean to deep-sea-and-sail.

RELIGION AND POLITICS

ALLEN, J. W.: *Political Thought in the Sixteenth Century.*
ARMSTRONG, EDWARD: *The French Wars of Religion: Their Political Aspects.*
BAYNE, C. G.: *Anglo-Papal Relations, 1558–1566.*
CODE, JOSEPH BERNARD: *Queen Elizabeth and the English Catholic Historians.*
DIXON, R. W.: *History of the Church of England from the Abolition of the Roman Jurisdiction.*
FOXE, JOHN: *Actes and Monuments.*
FRERE, W. H.: *The English Church in the Reigns of Elizabeth and James I.*
FROUDE, JAMES ANTHONY: *The Spanish Story of the Armada.*
GLADISH, DOROTHY M.: *The Tudor Privy Council.*
HALLAM, HENRY: *Constitutional History of England.*
HUME, M. A. S.: *Treason and Plot: Struggles for Catholic Supremacy in the Last Years of Queen Elizabeth.*

INNES, ARTHUR D.: *England under the Tudors.*
KNAPPEN, MARSHALL MASON: *Tudor Puritanism.*
MEISSBERGER, L. ARNOLD: "Machiavelli and Tudor England" (*Political Science Quarterly*, vol. 42, Columbia University Press, 1927).
MEYER, A. O.: *England and the Catholic Church under Queen Elizabeth.*
NEALE, J. E.: *Elizabeth I and Her Parliaments.*
———: *The Age of Catherine de Medici.*
———: *The Elizabethan House of Commons.*
PERCY, LORD EUSTACE: *The Privy Council under the Tudors.*
POLLARD, A. F.: *Political History of England, 1547-1603.*
POLLEN, JOHN HUNGERFORD: *The English Catholics in the Reign of Queen Elizabeth, 1558-1580.*
PRAZ, DR. MARIO: "Machiavelli and the Elizabethans" (*Proceedings of the British Academy*, Oxford, 1923).
READ, CONYERS: *The Tudors: Personalities and Practical Politics in Sixteenth Century England.*
TAWNEY, R. H.: *Religion and the Rise of Capitalism.*
TYTLER, P. F.: *England under the Reigns of Edward VI and Mary.*

There might be those today who would think the coupling of these two subjects sacrilegious, or at any rate in poor taste. No Elizabethan would have thought so. In practice it was found impossible to separate them without great confusion. The literature here is enormous; and what is given above is meant to be no more than representative.

THE TIMES

CAMDEN, CARROLL: *The Elizabethan Woman.*
CAMDEN, WILLIAM: *Annals.*
CREIGHTON, MANDELL: *The Age of Elizabeth.*

DAVIS, WILLIAM STEARNS: *Life in Elizabethan Days.*
FURNIVALL, J. F., *see* HARRISON, WILLIAM.
HARRISON, G. B.: *An Elizabethan Journal.*
HARRISON, WILLIAM: *Description of England,* ed. by J. F. Furnivall.
HENTZNER, PAUL: *Travels in England, 1598.*
HOLINSHED, RICHARD: *Holinshed's Chronicles of England, Scotland, and Ireland.*
MELVILLE, SIR JAMES, OF HALHILL: *Memoirs of His Own Life.*
NICHOLS, JOHN: *The Progresses and Public Processions of Queen Elizabeth.*
POLLARD, A. F. (ed.): *Tudor Tracts.*
RALEIGH, WALTER (ed.): *Shakespeare's England.*
ROWSE, A. L.: *An Elizabethan Garland.*
——: *The England of Elizabeth.*
SPALDING, ALFRED: *Elizabethan Demonology.*
STOW, JOHN: *Annals.*
STUBBES, PHILIP: *Anatomie of the Abuses in England.*
SUMMERSON, JOHN: *Architecture in Britain, 1530 to 1830.*
TILLYARD, E. M. M.: *The Elizabethan World Picture.*
WILSON, JOHN DOVER: *Life in Shakespeare's England.*

Some of these—the Camden *Annals,* Stubbes, Stow, Holinshed, Nichols, etc.—are not always accessible to the layman; and indeed they are sometimes regarded almost as museum pieces rather than library books. Two more recent publications are warmly recommended—*Shakespeare's England,* a learned compilation, and Rowse's altogether admirable *The England of Elizabeth.* Of course, Shakespeare himself must always be the best source.

INDEX

Act of Uniformity, the, 85
Alençon, Duke of, *see* François de Valois
Alva, Fernando Álvarez de Toledo, Duke of, 41, 86–7, 92, 94, 106, 109, 111, 112, 123, 126, 135, 145, 171
Americas, 4, 20, 145
Angoulême, Charles d'Orléans, Duke of, 26
Angus, Archibald, Eighth Earl of, 74
Anjou, Henri, Duke of, later Henri III of France, 102, 119–22, 127, 129, 140
Anne of Austria, 93–4
Arbroath, Lord (James Stewart, Earl of Arran), 98
Armada, the, 171, 173–9, 180–1, 183–5
Armada (second), 189
Arran, James Hamilton, Third Earl of, 26, 55–6, 71, 73, 98
Arundel, Henry Fitzalan, Twelfth Earl of, 109
Arundel, House of, 26
Ashley, Katherine, 11, 12
Asia, 145

Babington, Anthony, 164–5
Bacon, Sir Nicholas, 3, 107, 114
Beaumont, Francis, 3
"Beggars of the Sea," 83
Belgium, *see* Low Countries
Bertie, Peregrine, 172
Blount, Charles, Earl of Devonshire, 46
Boleyn, Ann, 6–8
Bond of Association, 157–8
Bordeaux, 131
Bothwell, James Hepburn, Fourth Earl of, 78–80, 96–8, 108
Brabant, 136
Brederode, Hendrik van, 124
Brussels, 30

Cabot, Sebastian, 81
Cadiz Raid, 175
Caesar, Julius, 3
Calais, 32–3, 148
Cambridgeshire, 32
Campion, Edmund, 146–7
Carey, Henry, Lord Hunsdon, 110, 189
Carey, Robert, 192
Carlisle, 104

Index

Carlos de Austria, Don, 25, 40, 61–2
Castelnau, Michel de, Sieur de la Mauvissière, 147
Catherine of Aragon, 6, 14, 16
Catherine de' Medici, 42–3, 56, 61–2, 98, 119–22, 127–31, 146, 149, 188
Catholicism, 16, 30, 35–6, 39, 59, 66, 70, 72, 74, 76, 80, 81–3, 85, 95, 96, 100–1, 103–4, 105–7, 117, 124–6, 131, 136–9, 144, 147, 155–8, 162, 165, 167, 172, 180–1, 188–9
Cawood, Margaret, 79
Cecil, Robert, 52, 172, 190–1
Cecil, William, 47, 48, 51–3, 56, 58, 68, 107, 120, 125, 137, 154, 162, 165, 168, 186, 189–91
Chamberlin, Frederick, 35
Charles, Archduke of Austria, 59–61, 119–20
Charles V, King of Spain (Charles I, Holy Roman Emperor), 20, 22, 61, 84–5
Charles IX, King of France, 56, 61–2, 119–21, 128–30, 135
Chartley Manor, 162–3, 165
Chartres, de, 120
Châtillon, Sébastien, 120
Chelsea, 11, 12, 13

Cheshunt, 12
Clemens, Samuel Langhorne, 9
Clement VII, Pope, 14
Cleopatra, 3
Clifford, Margaret, 15
Coligny, Gaspard de, 128–30, 157
Columbus, Christopher, 4
Counter Reformation, 85
Courtenay, Edward, Earl of Devonshire, 25, 31
Cranmer, Thomas, Archbishop of Canterbury, 7

Darnley, Henry Stewart, Lord, 74–9, 108, 116, 133, 156
Dauphin of France, 41, 42; see also Francis II
Davison, William, 168
Denmark, 39, 80, 185
Derby, Henry Stanley, Fourth Earl of, 109
Desmond, House of, 133
Devereux, Robert, Earl of Essex, 64, 133, 190
Devonshire, 25
Douglas, William, of Lochleven, 97–8
Dover, 124
Drake, Sir Francis, 4–5, 88–90, 124, 144, 173–8, 184, 186, 189
Dudley, Robert, Earl of Leicester, 46, 48, 51, 52,

INDEX

Dudley, Robert (*continued*)
63–9, 75, 107, 120, 142, 148, 170–1, 181, 186–7
Dumbarton, 56, 97, 134

East Indies, 145
Edinburgh, 77, 78, 134
Edward I, King of England, 54
Edward VI, King of England, 8, 9, 10, 14–15, 36, 50, 81
Edward, Earl of Carnarvon, 54
Elizabeth I, Queen of England: parentage, 6–7; life with Katherine Parr and Tom Seymour, 8, 11–12; return to Hatfield, 12–13; death of Edward VI, 14; learning, 3, 14, 15, 115, 189–90; not visionary, 4, 136, 174; cautious with money, 4–5, 96, 111, 150, 155, 171–2, 178, 186, 188; attitudes toward religion, 16, 50, 64, 85, 100–1, 122; appearance, 18, 34, 150, 152–3; relationship with Mary Tudor, 16, 19, 32; marriage negotiations, 26–7, 59–62, 66–7, 118–23, 127, 139–49; evasiveness, 27, 48–9, 59–62, 68, 84, 90–1, 94, 96, 99, 100, 122;

Elizabeth I (*continued*)
140, 167–8, 191; political astuteness, 27–8; ascends to throne, 34; temper and sarcasm, 34, 41, 48, 64, 115, 189–90, 190; love of amusement and display, 48, 50, 66–7, 72–3, 152–3, 191; hard-working, 50, 151; conflict with Mary, Queen of Scots, 58, 72–5, 104–5, 116–18, 134, 158–9, 160; affair with Dudley, 63–9, 75; policy in Ireland, 70; seizure of Spanish treasure, 91–4; charm, 115; Ridolfi plot, 125–7; courtship of Duke of Alençon, 139—49; Babington conspiracy, 164–5; trial and execution of Mary, Queen of Scots, 166–8; Spanish Armada, 174–85; death of Robert Dudley, 186; death of Elizabeth, 192
Elizabeth of France, 41, 86, 93, 119, 121
Emmanuel Phillibert of Savoy, 26–7
English Channel, 6, 14, 21, 126, 131, 175
Eric XIV, King of Sweden, 26, 59
Essex, 32
Este, House of, 26

Falmouth, 87
Felton, John, 112–13
Fénélon, François de la Mothe, 122, 127, 132
Ferdinand, Archduke of Austria, 59–60
Ferdinand I, King of Austria, 59–61
Feria, de (Spanish Ambassador), 39–41, 91
Ferrara, House of, 26
Flanders, 136
Fletcher, John, 3
Foix, Paul de, 62
Ford, John, 3
Forth, Firth of, 184
Fotheringay, 166–8
France, 14, 15, 21, 26, 33, 39, 40, 42, 43, 58, 70, 81, 83, 84, 87, 95, 98, 102, 103, 104, 107, 112, 117, 121, 127–32, 135, 138, 144, 146–8, 154, 156, 159, 168, 171, 176, 188
Francis I, King of France, 26, 55, 119
Francis II, King of France, 108, 119
François de Valois, Duke of Alençon, 119, 127, 135–6, 139–49
Frobisher, Sir Martin, 4, 184

Gaul (Caesar), 3
Gelderland, 136
Genoa, 87
Germany, 136, 154, 156
Gifford, Gilbert, 162–3
Gilbert, Sir Humphrey, 81, 133
Glasgow, 78
Greenwich, 5, 18, 147, 151
Gregory XIII, Pope, 131, 138, 157
Gresham, Sir Thomas, 37
Grey, Lady Catherine, 44, 45, 64
Grey, Lady Jane, 15–17, 30, 44
Guaras, Antonio de, 156
Guinea, 89
Guise, Henri de Lorraine, Duke of, 33, 129, 155, 157, 158, 188
Guise, House of, 42, 43, 57, 95, 102, 117, 121, 128–9, 134, 138, 146, 167, 171

Habsburg, House of, 14, 21, 23, 60, 61, 84, 120
Hainault, 136
Hamilton, House of, 55, 74, 95, 97–8, 133
Hamlet (Shakespeare), 53
Hampton Court, 5, 72, 151
Hatfield, 12–14, 16, 18, 25, 28, 32, 33, 59, 151, 167
Hatton, Christopher, 46, 142, 189
Havre, Le, 148
Hawkins, John, 89–90

INDEX

Henry, King of Portugal, 145
Henri II, King of France, 41–2, 86
Henri III, King of France, 135, 146–8, 157, 167, 188
Henri of Navarre, 119, 127, 135, 188–9
Henry VII, King of England, 42, 54
Henry VIII, King of England, 3, 6–11, 14–16, 24, 36, 41, 54, 81, 118
Herries, John Maxwell, Lord, 98
Hertford, Edward Seymour, Earl of, 44–5
Hertfordshire, 32
Holland, see Low Countries
Howard, Charles, Baron Howard of Effingham, 173–4, 184, 186
Howard, Katherine, 8
Huguenots, 43, 57, 61, 83, 102, 117, 120, 127–31, 148, 155
Hunsdon, Lord, see Henry Carey

Inquisition, Spanish, 24, 125
Ireland, 6, 39, 70, 102, 111, 123, 133, 145, 185, 186
Irish Sea, 185
Italy, 86, 92, 119
Ivan IV, Tsar of Russia, 26

James I, King of England, 48, 64, 77, 96, 105, 116, 134, 158, 161, 167, 169, 172, 184, 191, 192
James V, King of Scotland, 42, 55, 78, 97
Jesuits, 85, 107, 137, 138, 163, 180
Jones, Inigo, 18
Jonson, Ben, 3

Kent, 32

Langside, 98
Latimer, Hugh, 31
Leith, 56–7, 134
Lennox, Matthew Stewart, Earl of, 133, 157
Lennox, Margaret Douglas, Countess of, 74
Linlithgow, 79
Lisbon, 145, 175–6
Lochleven, 80, 86, 95, 97
London, 18, 24, 27, 56, 62, 72, 104, 108, 112, 125, 126, 134, 151, 166, 176, 177, 181–2
Louis of Nassau, 136
Low Countries, 14, 20, 39, 40, 43, 81, 83, 84–7, 92–3, 103, 106, 124–5, 127–8, 135–6, 144, 146, 148, 154, 156, 157, 170, 171, 177, 185
Luxembourg, 136
Lyons, 131

Maitland, William, 74-5
Mar, John Erskine, Earl of, 160
Margaret of France, 119, 128
Mary of Guise, 39, 43
Mary of Lorraine, 55, 57
Mary, Queen of Scots, 15, 39, 41-2, 55, 57-8, 61-2, 70-80, 86, 95-9, 104-10, 116-18, 121, 126, 134, 138, 158-68
Mary Tudor, Queen of England, 6, 8, 10, 15-16, 19, 21-2, 24-5, 28, 29-33, 36, 50, 51, 65, 95, 138, 140
Maximilian II, King of Hungary, 112
Meaux, 131
Medici, House of, 26
Medina-Sidonia, Alonso Pérez de Guzmán, Duke of, 178
Melville, Sir James, 72-3
Mendoza, Bernardino de, 145, 156
Middleton, Thomas, 3
Montgomery de Lorge, Count, 41, 52, 119
Morton, James Douglas, Earl of, 133
Murray, James Stewart, Earl of, 71, 95-6, 98, 105, 116-17, 133, 157

Nombre de Dios, 124
Nonesuch, 5, 18
Norfolk, Thomas, Duke of, 63, 74, 108-9, 126-7
Norman Conquest, 6, 54
Norris, Sir John, 170-2, 181
Northumberland, John Dudley, Duke of, 14-16, 109-10

Oatlands, 5, 18
O'Neil, Shane, 70
Orléans, 131
Oxenham, John, 124
Oxford, 142

Pacific Ocean, 124
Padua, 31
Page (pamphleteer), 142-3
Pagnozzo, Roberto Ridolfi di, 125-6
Paris, 58, 117, 127-31, 146, 189
Parliament, 24, 49, 52, 59, 111, 114, 116, 136, 167, 182, 190
Parma, Alessandro, Duke of, 157, 164, 171, 177, 181-2, 185
Parma, Margaret of, 43
Parr, Katherine, 8, 10, 11-12
Paulet, Sir Amyas, 159, 161-3, 168

INDEX

Peterborough Cathedral, 168
Phelippes, Thomas, 163–5
Philip II, King of Spain, 20–8, 30–2, 39–41, 45, 50, 57, 61, 66–7, 84–7, 89–90, 92–3, 100, 102, 106, 112, 114, 119, 121, 123–5, 127, 131, 134–5, 140, 145, 155–8, 161, 173, 176–9, 181, 189
Pickering, Sir William, 65
Pius IV, Pope, 39, 66, 75, 101, 103
Pius V, Pope, 105, 106, 108, 112, 119, 125
Plantagenets, 54, 73
Plymouth, 87, 174, 176, 179
Pole, Reginald, 22
Portugal, 83, 115, 145, 171
Prince and the Pauper, The (Twain), 9
Protestantism, 35–6, 55–6, 59, 61, 74, 82–3, 96, 100–2, 104, 108–9, 112, 135–6, 154, 158, 166, 177

Quadra, Bishop de, 61, 66–7, 91, 100

Raleigh, Sir Walter, 44, 46, 67, 142, 187, 190
Reformation, Protestant, 85
Requeséns, Luis de Zúñiga y, 135
Richmond, 151

Ridley, Nicholas, 31
Rising in the North, 106–10, 116–18, 120, 139, 180
Rizzio, David, 76–7, 156
Robsart, Amy, Lady Dudley, 68–9
Ross, Bishop of, 126
Rouen, 131
Rowley, William, 3
Russia, 39, 154

Sadler, Sir Ralph, 159, 161
St. Bartholomew massacres, 130–1, 140, 144, 160
St. Paul's Church, 112
San Juan de Ulloa (Veracruz), 90–1, 124
Santa Cruz, Álvaro de Bazán, 171, 176–8
Saxony, House of, 26
Scandinavia, 154
Scarborough Castle, 32
Scheldt River, 136
Scotland, 6, 14, 39, 43, 54–8, 70–3, 76, 79–80, 95–7, 103–4, 105, 108, 110, 117, 121, 123, 133, 146, 156, 160, 167
Scrope, Lady, 192
Seymour, Edward, Duke of Somerset, 9–10, 13, 14, 45
Seymour, Jane, 8, 9
Seymour, Thomas, Baron Seymour of Sudeley, 8–13, 26

Shakespeare, William, 3, 52–3
Sheffield, 105, 117, 160, 164
Shrewsbury, George Talbot, Earl of, 117, 159–60, 189
Silva, Diego de, 91, 114
Simier, Jean de, 141–2, 144
Singleton (printer), 142–3
Sixtus V, Pope, 172, 185
Smithfield burnings, 24
Solway Moss, Battle of, 42
Solway River, 42, 98–9, 116
Southampton, 87
Spain, 14, 17, 20, 21, 23, 39, 41, 61, 66, 67, 70, 82–4, 89, 92–4, 103, 107, 119, 123, 125, 127, 134, 135, 144, 145, 146, 154, 156, 167, 170–1, 173–8, 182–6, 189
Spies, Don Gerau de, 91–2, 125–6, 156
Stafford, Sir Thomas, 32
Stewart, House of, 47, 54
Stewart, Lord Robert, 78
Stubbs, John, 142–3
Sussex, 32
Sussex, Thomas Radcliffe, Earl of, 63, 109, 110, 120, 140
Sweden, 39
Switzerland, 56

Thames River, 5, 19, 66, 151, 182

Throckmorton, Elizabeth, 44
Throckmorton, Sir Nicholas, 31
Tilbury, 182
Toulon, 131
Tower of London, 7, 12, 19, 44, 63, 64, 88, 94, 109, 126, 145, 156, 168, 188
Treaty of Edinburgh, 58, 72, 73
Trent, 103
Trent, Council of, 138
Tudor, Margaret, 41, 54–5, 74
Tudors, 25, 54, 81, 114
Tutbury, 105, 110, 159, 161–2
Twain, Mark, pseudonym for Samuel Langhorne Clemens, *q.v.*
Tyrwhitt, Sir Robert, 12

Valois, House of, 86, 119, 122, 127, 135, 188
Vienna, 61, 120
Vitelli, Chapin, 93–4, 103

Wales, 6
Walsingham, Sir Francis, 34, 137, 140, 161–5, 189
Warwick, Ambrose, Earl of, 75, 189
Warwickshire, 32
Webster, John, 3
West Indies, 4, 20, 40, 84, 89

INDEX

Westminster, 143
Westmoreland, Charles Neville, Earl of, 109–10
Westmoreland, House of, 26
Whitehall, 5, 18, 19, 33
William of Orange, 102, 135, 136, 148–9, 157
Williams, Sir Roger, 172
Windsor, 5, 151
Wyatt Rebellion, 17, 25, 30, 35, 63, 74
Wynter, Sir William, 57

Zeeland, 136

www.ingramcontent.com/pod-product-compliance
Lightning Source LLC
LaVergne TN
LVHW041616070426
835507LV00008B/271